Provolution

A Guide to Global Change Through Your Personal Evolution

Provolution

A Guide to Global Change Through Your Personal Evolution

Michael Stephens

BOOKS

Winchester, UK
Washington, USA

First published by O-Books, 2010
O Books is an imprint of John Hunt Publishing Ltd., The Bothy, Deershot Lodge, Park Lane, Ropley, Hants, SO24 0BE, UK
office1@o-books.net
www.o-books.com

For distributor details and how to order please visit the 'Ordering' section on our website.

ISBN: 978 1 84694 310 2

A CIP catalogue record for this book is available from the British Library.

Design: Stuart Davies

Printed in the UK by CPI Antony Rowe
Printed in the USA by Offset Paperback Mfrs, Inc

CONTENTS

Dedication

Dedicated to Koong, Jacob and Aine. Thank you for grounding me here and now. Thank you for reminding me to observe when I react. Thank you for asking questions of my i-go that I could never ask alone. I love you and am grateful for all you teach me everyday.

Preface

Writing this book has taught me that practice makes perfect and that writing changes nothing. Knowing what I know is not the same as doing what I should or could be doing.

It has also taught me that I need to buy a new chair.

People ask me what "Provolution" means and why we need new words to say what we want to say. Provolution has taught me that our whole mental state is hot-wired into everything from our systems to our physical products. Not the least of these is the language that we use in our day-to-day lives. We need new words to describe what we dream of doing if the old ones don't inspire us to go where we need to go. Perhaps then we will find the energy to actually get there.

Provolution has been a labor of love and there are many I love who I must thank for this work. I am lucky in that I share my world with a great many great people on Phuket, Thailand who are provolving in all kinds of inspiring ways as wonderful healers, therapists and teachers.

In the last five years I have been awed and humbled to know Roger Moore, Dorinda Rose Berry and Nikorn Banderlert , Jason Blackman, Bill Gould, Pat Thummanond, Rhonda Ann Clarke (out of sight but not out of mind) and many others, and want to thank them sincerely for all the learning we have done together and for the learning still to come.

I also want to honor my parents, David and Deana for bringing me into this world, teaching me everything they knew and giving me the best they could with what they had. This is all anyone can do. I want to express my sincere love, gratitude and appreciation for how easy you made it seem to be good at what, I have come to learn, is neither easy nor routine. I am privileged to be your son and thank you for being my parents.

Finally, I also want to thank Kirstie Flood and Jason, once

again, for their proofreading and for making me realize the first three chapters didn't need to change the world.

That's ***your*** job.

Be well.

MS

www.provolutionthebook.com

Introduction

"Everyone thinks of changing the world, but no one thinks of changing himself."
Leo Tolstoy – Russian Writer (1828–1910)

Provolution means the positive evolution of human consciousness. It is not about overthrowing governments, battling evil or throwing off the yoke of oppression. Indeed, it has nothing at all to do with changing the world outside of you, and everything to do with creating evolution inside of you. It defines a movement towards revelation of who you really are and a profound understanding of your spiritual nature.

As much as conventional thought insists the world to be an objective place where your freedom is built from physical truth and the stuff you find in shopping malls, the vast subjective jungle lying unexplored inside you is the only truth that really matters. The final frontier of human exploration is the space between your ears for the freedom you seek is not a real place. It is not a real time. You can neither buy it, hold it, nor measure it. It is a place discovered through sensitivity and awareness, by listening to the silence of the real you who hides beneath the chatter of inner voices claiming that you already know who you are.

When you open your heart to the true nature of reality, you will realize it is a place of contrasts, of love that binds all things together and of suffering that pulls all things apart. The current consciousness of humankind translates internal emotional suffering into the external violence we perpetrate against the planet and one another. But this is not a permanent condition. It can change if you change. Much of humanity's violent history is merely a physical reflection of a collective spiritual state. Provolution is about discovering the roots of the suffering within your human spirit so that you can fight the demons in your heart and not on physical battlefields.

Provolution is a call for peaceful global transformation through individual people. Within your own mind an onion skin of conditioning has obscured your sensitivity to the natural order of things. You have become cocooned within a bubble of awareness. Provolution will show you how to peel away these layers, to pop the bubble, belief by belief, concept by concept, and recognize the spiritual connections that transcend parochial human values, culture or law. You are not separate and independent from anything or anyone. You are not alone. You are a part of something far greater than you ever imagined. Though religions divide us into faiths, governments split us into nationalities, companies define us as human-doings not human beings, Provolution throws off the artificial labels that have conditioned your perception of who you have become and encourages you to be who you really are.

Provolution is not a traditional workbook or meditation manual, although it contains many techniques that will steer you towards deeper practices. Neither is it a guide to spiritual enlightenment, although it will help you create an environment where anything becomes possible. It is an investigation into the conventional beliefs from which the personal and collective reality is most commonly built.

In Part I you will learn to create a healthy mind and body for yourself. You will understand how you have been conditioned to suffer through the learning you have accepted as your personal truth. By comparing and contrasting popular beliefs with the laws of nature you will comprehend how the global reality has been shaped by human ideas that are illusory, false and destructive to your personal wellbeing. You will discover how the connected thoughts and feelings that arise from these beliefs condition a cycle of suffering that translates into your physical body and the physical world around you. Part I will give you the skills and concepts to evolve beyond clinging to the world through i-go that perceives everything as 'I', 'me' and 'mine', and to reduce the spiral of suffering that may very well be creating the conditions for your physical sickness or death.

In Part II you will learn the significance of your personal spiritual nature. By delving into an insightful breakdown of elements comprising your human spirit you will learn how relationships between you and your family, neighborhood and city or state and country can be improved by meeting basic spiritual needs vital to all healthy relationships, while also understanding why so many relationships break down when these needs are not met. By looking at the spiritual connections between us all through the relational mirror and understanding the collective reality of we-go to which we all contribute, you will realize the interdependent nature of this universe and why it is imperative that all people wake up and contribute to the global transformation in a positive manner if we are going to evolve as a species.

Part II will demonstrate to you why expanding the spiritual connection of people to one another is the greatest challenge to humanity's future survival, but also why an emerging trend towards greater human spirituality is the ultimate solution to the global, social and environmental problems we face today.

I make no apologies for being a seeker of truth, and in the process have come to understand just how ridiculous the whole premise of truth really is. My spirituality has been learned the hard way, through ups and downs, highs and lows, trial and error. By virtue of this I believe my experience will assist the multitudes of people who find the process of transformation as hard as I do. After spending the last 20 years seeking to understand the mysteries of life and applying them to make a better reality for myself and others around me, this book is a collection of the best ways I have found thus far; ways that have worked for me.

From retreats in India in the early 1990's to being a wellness teacher and practitioner in Thailand today, I have come to know that provolution is not for the faint of heart. It is a brave step to desire change and it is inevitable that some readers will find this journey painful for it strikes at the very core of what you believe to be true and untrue. I urge perseverance. If I transfer some of my passion to the reader, translated into a sense of urgency, I apologize in advance. I hope it serves as good preparation for the trials of transformation that lie ahead. You are a seeker of peace, but I know of no other path towards it than challenging the truth you currently hold inside you and holding it up to the light as the sole cause of your suffering. You must challenge it as passionately as you know how. Needless to say, this is not always a pleasant experience, as I can attest to. My current contentment results from a painful expansion of my awareness, a dramatic transformation of what I believed to be true in this world and a reconnection to the universe so far from where I began that my perception of reality was turned inside out and upside down. Some people are just not ready for what this means but, as my mother says, you can't make an omelet without breaking eggs. The smashing of a few personal truths is where your journey of provolution is headed too because it is a journey beyond the way things seem and into what they really are. In this book, there are no sacred cows.

To end your suffering takes a little risk. It takes a little effort. It takes a little time. But, when the dust settles and you rub the sleep from your eyes, you will find yourself in a landscape where the effort was worthwhile and the view spectacular. It is time to let go of who you think you are and embrace a new you. It is a risk, of course, but when you risk it all and win, you end up with more than you ever imagined possible. Suddenly, something beyond the limits of your own perception is brought into clarity and nothing ever seems impossible again.

I have not written this book to fight anyone, condemn

anything or win any arguments about what is real and what is not. I am not here to prove me right or anyone else wrong. In my experience, struggling to adapt the entire world to my personal beliefs and preferences has been a forlorn task. I cannot change you. I cannot change the nature of reality. I can only adapt me to the true nature of the world around me. And that's plenty. It took me too long to realize that I could rave at the economic situation all I liked, become furious at the social inequality, rant at the political ineptitude I see every day, but I merely ended up furious, ranting and raving. That's of no use to the peace seeker. My hope is that Provolution will help you to understand this learning just a little quicker than I did.

It is more love that we need in this world as from love cascades the compassion, respect, trust, and dignity from which healthy relationships and communities grow quite naturally. Only through inclusivity can we breach the walls we have erected to protect us without thought of the view that we fill with bricks or the shadows that they cast across our lives. My sincerest hope is that Provolution will provide you with enough light to banish a few of those shadows and realize the seamless interdependence of your own reality with everything and everyone else's. When each of us accepts and assumes the responsibility for our part in creating the world we share, it ***will*** change. The awesome personal power that we all possess transforms the world one person at a time.

Part I: Provolution of Mind and Body

Chapter 1

Self-Awareness

"We are here and it is now. Further than that all human knowledge is moonshine."
H. L. Mencken – American Journalist and Satirist (1880 - 1956)

Awareness vs. Knowledge

Are you aware? If you think you are, ask how aware you are of your own self. How often do you listen to your mind, to your body, to your emotions, to the real you compressed beneath myriad ideas and beliefs that claim to be you? It is not something that the majority of us are taught to do, is it? Particularly in the West, we believe we have a natural knowledge of self but this is the grandest of illusions. We have learned so much about the outside world that awareness of the internal world seems comparatively insignificant. However, in these challenging times of global interconnectivity and volatility, there is a pressing need to seek alternative solutions to stubborn problems that just don't seem to go away using traditional methods. Perhaps the problems we are trying to solve are not outside of us at all but within minds that must rediscover why self-awareness was once such a vital tool in the human quest for survival.

Many of us may subscribe to the notion that *'Knowledge is power'*, Sir Francis Bacon's preferred view of life, but this is an illusion of power. The true power you need to assume control of your life stems from your sensitivity to the present moment. This is called mindfulness. If you imagine that your mind is a machine full of emotional switches that have been put in place by the learning you have accumulated throughout your life, an unmindful person turns the machine to automatic, running their life according to learned emotional reactions arising with every experience in their life. If you have ever made a bad decision in anger, you will know how painful a life like this can be. However, it is no less painful than a bad decision made in love, is it?

Whether we perceive an emotion to be positive or negative, whichever emotions we react to, the result is rarely positive. But this is how most people live, in unmindful reaction to events. On the other hand, a mindful person is aware of and takes responsibility for all their emotions as they arise. They can carefully select their course of action because they do not get emotionally involved in events. While many of us might claim that this sounds like the recipe to become a robot or emotionless zombie, in fact the opposite is true. When you observe events, you are in control of them. When you simply react in a preconditioned way, passively allowing emotional switches to flip, this is robotic. Observing and not reacting means taking responsibility for how you feel, not ***becoming*** how you feel. Mindful action will always create a better quality of life than unmindful reaction and we will be exploring in this section how personal dedication to the former will create a foundation of personal awareness from which a new world of potential opens up to you.

What use is all the knowledge you acquire in life if it does not help you to create a reality that ***feels*** better? You and every other person on earth are seeking exactly the same thing from life: freedom from your suffering. You want to ***feel good***. You want ***contentment***. Some may call this liberty, others may call it peace but whatever you call it, the incredible reality is that everyone is actually seeking nothing more than a ***still mind***. It is hardly the first solution we embrace, is it? This may account for why so few of us actually find contentment.

While religion, entertainment or physical pleasures are the most common avenues of exploration in our search for peace, none tackle the root cause of suffering, which is the same in all cases: the mind. Your mind is the creator of everything you do in life as well as everything that you feel. Being able to identify how contentment arises and what is preventing it requires a mind that is trained to investigate reality. You need to become Sherlock Holmes seeking the perpetrator of suffering inside your own head in order to capture peace but if you have not trained yourself to be the perceptive, sensitive, aware solution finder what have your trained yourself to be? The ordinary mind is rarely able to identify itself as the cause of its own suffering. If we learned to still the mind, not animate it, we could observe its true state of clinging and attachment to ideas that promote and expand suffering and in the practice of stilling it contentment would arise naturally. But to catch the mind in animation and learn how to still it, we must develop mental awareness and practice it throughout our day. Herein lies the problem.

Our modern recipe for contentment prescribes the polar opposite of stilling the mind. We keep it occupied in order that its true nature remains obscured. It is a bitter irony that the occupied mind, while believing it possesses an identity characterized by the passing thoughts, feelings and opinions floating through it, is actually a kind of spiritual imposter, cloaking the true you with a series of associated thoughts that maintain a fraudulent impression of who you think you are. We acquire knowledge and fulfill desires, forgoing awareness of the present moment or observation of the true self within us, thus ensuring that this imposter remains an uncomfortable bedfellow for as long as we remain ignorant of its presence. However, while we may be familiar with the daily head rush of thoughts and ideas buzzing around our brains, a still mind is no more natural to you than an animated mind. It has merely been repetitively practiced and reinforced within the culture, habits and peer behaviors of the society in which you grew up. Just as it has been learned, so it can be unlearned. Sensitivity to the world around you or the ability to observe your emotions rather than just mechanically react:

these are all components of wisdom but they are rarely cultivated as the essential ingredients of human contentment by any predominant learning institutions within mainstream Western society. Indeed, they are alien concepts to most of us. Rather, the mind is perceived as requiring the food of knowledge to nurture it, like your car requires fuel to run but, while great knowledge is important, what good does it do you if you do not possess the sensitivity to choose wisely, humanely, lovingly to create contentment for yourself and others with whom you share your reality? This wisdom is another aspect of awareness that is rarely considered. If we simply chase contentment and do not consider why we are discontent in the first place, we risk adding fuel to the very fire that burns us.

The British biologist Thomas H. Huxley hit the nail on the head when he said, *"If a little knowledge is dangerous, where is the man who has so much as to be out of danger."* We cannot learn our way out of suffering while repeating the same habits and behaviors that caused us to suffer in the first place. Indeed, the greatest danger of all may be realized through our unflinching faith that the more knowledge we have, the less danger we are in when the opposite may be true. Intellectual conceit leads to moral conceit which soon creates such a sense of superiority that we feel justified to commit unconscionable acts that have nothing to do with our contentment or anyone else's. William Shockley, American Nobel Prize winner and inventor of the transistor, one of the most intuitive and transformational creations of the twentieth century, was clearly a very knowledgeable individual but he spent the latter years of his life promoting a program of sterilization based upon IQ! You see, there is no intellectual substitute for compassion and compassion cannot be taught through books or mere comprehension of what it is. Compassion must be ***experienced*** before it becomes a learned trait. Moreover, anyone of any intellect can be compassionate. Caring power is not a matter of brainpower. However much we know, a failure to *feel* the human connection and responsibility of one person to the next, and each of us to the whole, rejects empathy and compassion as moderators of our actions and people suddenly become capable of the unthinkable.

The focus on knowledge development as opposed to awareness development is an ideological choice that has a deep social impact. In education it creates a system focused on knowledge retention and preparing people for a successful career. This is not designed for the higher purpose of individual contentment, community or self-expression. The emotional, creative or relational aspects of human nature are often entirely ignored in favor of what can more easily be measured and tested. How do you test compassion, love, empathy or the ability to care? We have focused the purpose of our learning systems on the transfer of knowledge, not the expansion of sensitivity and awareness and this leaves adults in a position where we suspect our personal suffering to be a result of the wrong information, the wrong possessions or the wrong job or social status. It is none of those things. If we are unaware of our internal self, we are rendered impotent to cultivate the wisdom to realize where the problem of contentment both begins and ends.

Experiential Learning

Fifty thousand years ago, our ancestral tribes of nomads would have survived or died out according to the degree of self-awareness and sensitivity to the environment they attained in their lives. Experiential learning through daily experience would have assumed the role of knowledge transfer that epitomizes the 21st century's learning systems. Nomadic tribes did not have the luxury of refrigerated foods, government benefits, or home plumbing for their water, therefore survival would have been dependent upon getting what they needed when they needed it. Up-to-the-minute sensitivity to the passage of the sun, the tides of the sea, the seasons of the year, migration and breeding cycles of animals, growth cycles of plants, seasonal fruit, berries and nuts, weather, etc. would have occurred as a matter of course as people became naturally entrained with their environment because their very survival depended upon it.

Those nomads who were most sensitive and aware of their environment would have survived longest. If a child grew up in fear of the forest, for example, and was unable to address that fear, it would surely be his undoing. Fear is a projection of the future, not of the present reality and is therefore a poor survival tool. While many of us may perceive a forest to be a daunting place full of dark trees and dangerous animals, this is more a projection of our modern fears than how you would have felt were you raised in a nomadic environment. Tribal survival depended upon experiential learning in the real world and application under pressure, in the present moment. Children were thrust into the wild to learn these skills, maturing quickly by partnering and assisting their adult teachers, learning by doing and intensely experiencing their environment so that they could perfect the crafts that would keep them alive and prospering. Success was founded upon mastering feelings as they arose and making profound decisions under extreme environmental pressures hunting, fighting, scavenging, and seeking resources based upon real-world experience of nature's patterns, tendencies and behaviors. In the forest, knowing the names and species of every snake doesn't keep you alive. If you meet one, being experienced in the nature of the snake, sensitive to its presence on the path and acting with mindfulness is the best mechanism for survival. Therefore, it is important to understand how, to the nomadic mind, sensitivity to the outside world and awareness of the inside world were synonymous. Unlike modern people, not only did the nomad connect his personal nature to the natural environment, he also intimately understood the inseparable bond that connected his future with that of the environment in which he lived.

The Spiral of Learning

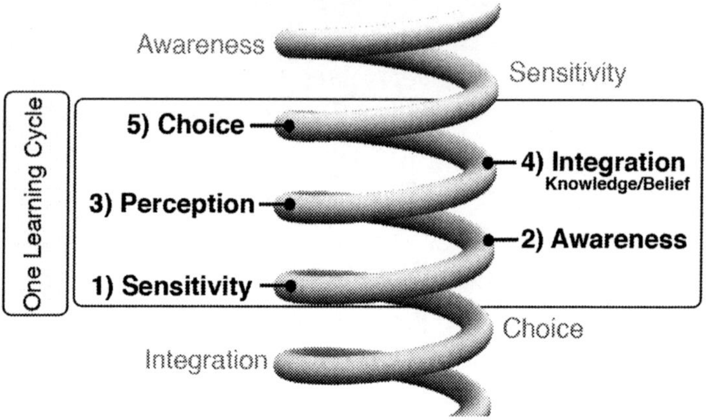

This type of experiential learning is rare these days, although the trend is, thankfully, changing a little. All learning occurs in a cycle of five phases: sensitivity, awareness, perception, integration into memory and belief systems and, last but not least, choice. Knowledge is just one part of the fourth stage and by leaping past the first three stages modern learning systems reduce the significance of sensitivity, awareness and perception as tools that enhance adaptability and therefore human prospects for survival and contentment.

Applications of knowledge: science, business and political systems, may have given rise to awe-inspiring technologies but they can hardly claim to have discovered the fountain of human contentment. While often being flaunted as the poster boy of human 'civilization' and 'progress' they also mask a downward trend in human awareness that has a disturbing inverse correlation with the upward trend in ecological and social disintegration that has accelerated so rapidly since the early 1900's and particularly since the 1970's.

Herbert Spencer coined the phrase *"survival of the fittest"* and by use of the word 'fittest' Spencer wasn't just referring to physical prowess. He was referring to a species' adaptability too.

A highly adaptable life form will be highly sensitized to its environment. It will live in the present moment dealing with what occurs as it occurs. This allows it to quickly adjust behavior in real time. In such circumstances, you don't have time to think, to analyze, to weigh up pros and cons or to SWOT analyze. Reaction must be in rhythm with the challenge: proportionate and appropriate. The quicker a life form can adjust its behavior to meet the needs of the changes it detects, the more likely it is to survive them. Thus the key to adaptability is the awareness of the changing environment. If life is unable to change or it adapts too slowly, it will die out.

The tribal nomad would have been perfectly honed as an adaptable being, but today many modern people have become creatures of habit and routine, disconnected from their own emotional state and connected to artificial stimuli that teach them nothing but conditioned reactions. We have lost our connection to nature and the present moment and therefore the sensitivity to our own feelings and emotions as they arise within us. We are taught to think, not to feel and thus our species has shifted from being heart-centered to head-centered where economics and balance sheets guide us, not gut feelings and intuition. It is not coincidental that this shift has ushered in a startling rise in psychological trauma and related physical disease in our modern societies. In urban jungles, not natural ones, cocooned from the natural patterns that would normally entrain a person to the nurturing rhythms and cycles of life, people become lost and disconnected from their own nature without any effort at all. We naturally become entrained to human-made patterns that condition us with artificial habits prone to inhibit feelings, causing many to turn anger inwards and create anxiety or depression because we are not centered in the present, grounded in the now or aware of from where or why these painful feelings arise. We have not learned the basic survival tools of our ancestors, the survival tools that would likewise naturally evolve us beyond the suffering inherent within the very concept of urbanized societies. We live in a human jungle of past and future, divided from the here and now, where all lessons are communicated and learned.

This disconnection leads us directly to humanity's most pressing problem.

In 1973, Dr. Grossarth-Maticek conducted a self-regulation test with almost six thousand 40-66 year-old participants from Heidelberg, Germany. The test measured, on a scale of 1-6 (1 = low), how aware people were of the results of their behavior and how responsible they were for adapting it to reduce the mental negativity it caused in their life and maximize a positive sense of wellbeing. Fifteen years later the results of the test showed, quite incredibly, that only 1.6 per cent of respondents who scored lower than two were still alive while 86 per cent of those who scored above five were still alive. Even more amazingly, the lifestyle of the respondents seemed to be less of a factor in their survival than their sensitivity to the existence of their problems and the related ability to adapt their mindset to be more positive. For at least 10 years before testing, approximately 300 of the respondents who achieved a score above five had smoked more than 20 cigarettes a day, drank more than the recommended alcohol limit, ate an unhealthy diet and did little or no exercise. Despite this, these 300 people outlived the group with poor self-regulation scores by an average of 8.5 years! Putting this into layman's terms, Dr. Grossarth-Maticek showed that popping pills, applying lotions or chopping out damaged body parts does not guarantee physical wellbeing because the causes of human sickness are not removed by removing the symptoms. Astonishingly, wellbeing is most effectively created through the simplest of processes: sensitivity to who you are and willingness to adapt the behaviors that create and recreate who you are.

Dr. Grossarth-Maticek's study reflects the current challenges facing humanity with stark clarity, the most obvious of which is redefining how wellness is generated and of teaching people to be sensitive and aware of who they are in the present moment. As we shall learn in later chapters, this is a scientifically proven requirement of good physical and mental health as well as longevity and quality of life. Yet it also blares a sobering warning for our entire species. The individual is a reflection of the species and the species a reflection of the individual and while Dr. Grossarth-Maticek's study clearly demonstrates that a person who is unable to avoid suffering by adapting habits and behaviors will surely perish prematurely, so too can we assume that the same is true for our entire species. If we do not once again learn to be sensitive and aware of those habits and behaviors that are harming us individually, our species faces premature extinction. How much longer can we continue building walls around our lives, creating toxic environments, generating relational conflicts and stifling the self-awareness that offers true liberty from the conditions we have created socially and environmentally? The answer, according to the current state of this planet, is 'not much longer'. Change must start now. And it must start with you.

Whenever my wife or I talk with a client who attends one of our workshops or healing sessions, the issues that emerge are always associated with awareness. There is no other problem facing people today. You cannot solve a problem you are unaware of. Often people will complain that this problem or that problem is bothering them and they don't know what to do about it but the answer we give is always the same: *"Awareness that you have a problem is such a huge leap to have taken. Just imagine the mess you'd be in if you were unaware where all of that suffering was coming from?"* This brings with it a kind of relief all of its own and a starting point for provolution in your life. If you have identified problems, fantastic! You don't yet realize how massive that step is. The next step is to commit to a process of mental transformation to remove the root causes of the problem, which will translate into physical habits and behaviors. This will bring different challenges all together, as we will be discussing in the next chapter.

Awareness is the key to your personal provolution because it raises your sensitivity to who you are and what is going on inside you. Just as a good doctor wouldn't operate on a patient without having a thorough understanding of anatomy and physiology and having done some solid physical investigation beforehand (I hope!), so your initial task is to undertake some solid investigation into the root cause of your problems: your mind. Without awareness of how the mind works, what you believe and how thoughts arise without any warning through the conditions you have created for yourself, how can you ever know what part of you needs to be 'operated on' in order to remove the root of your problems?

By realizing that awareness trumps knowledge in the game of wellbeing, you are setting out a new stall of values for yourself that aligns you with the potential to create lasting change in your reality. This leads us to question where your beliefs and values have come from in the first place and how they can evolve further. In the same way that we have looked back at our ancestors in this chapter and wondered what is implied by our lost awareness and disconnection from natural cycles, now we must begin expanding our awareness once again by investigating from where our beliefs are derived and the illusion of truth on which our minds obsess.

Yet let's just pause one last time to imagine the awareness and sensitivity our nomadic ancestors would have acquired in comparison with modern people today. They may not have possessed as much technical knowledge as we do but they were in communion with nature, sensitive to its every whim, and adaptation would have been a natural process to them. Somehow we must find a middle way between knowledge and awareness where sensitivity and awareness practice is no longer a fringe activity but perceived as a vital element of human wellbeing that opens up hearts to new paths and directions. If we can expand our sensitivity to our essential nature and expand this out to others around us, our applications of knowledge will then have a higher purpose that recognizes, with all the wisdom of our ancestors, that without awareness of and sensitivity to the shifting state of our minds there can be no wisdom in our world at all.

Chapter 2

Mind Rafts

"Most people grow old within a small circle of ideas, which they have not discovered for themselves."

Luc de Clapiers, marquis de Vauvenargues, French Moralist and Writer (1715 –1747)

The Parable of the Raft

A great teacher was traveling around an ancient country teaching as he passed from village to village. During his travels a gnarly skeptic attached himself to his traveling posse of disciples and made it his personal mission to heckle the teacher wherever he went. After each lesson, being of a compassionate nature, the teacher would routinely call upon the heckler to ask his skeptical questions, knowing that other people may have the same questions on their mind but may be too gentle-hearted to ask.

One night, the heckler lay awake for many hours devising a devilish question that he was sure would embarrass the teacher in front of his students. The next day, as was usual after his lesson, the teacher called on the heckler to speak whatever was on his mind and the heckler snapped back "Is your way the only way, teacher? Are you telling us you possess the ***only truth?"*** *The teacher instantly recognized another of the heckler's trick questions. He couldn't reply "Yes" because he knew that his way was just one way of many and he would never want to disrespect all the teachers who had taught him all the different ways that were each a small part of who he had become today. On the other hand, if he replied "No", the heckler would surely accuse him of teaching concepts that had no value, which he knew from personal experience was not the case.*

Rather than reply directly, the teacher thought for a moment before asking the heckler to consider a problem. He said: "Imagine that you had been journeying for many years, over many mountains, through many forests and across the many plains of this great and vast country and one day you came to the bank of a strong, wide river. The river is flowing too ferociously to swim across and the nearest bridge is so far away that it would take you many days to reach it on foot. You sit down under the refreshing shade of a bamboo thicket and think about the problem." Looking at the heckler as he digested the scenario, the teacher asked him, "How would you cross the river?"

The heckler thought carefully for a moment, knowing that the teacher was a cunning adversary in their daily ritual, before deciding that he would take his trusty machete from his pack, cut down the bamboo from the side of the river and build a raft bound together by the reeds growing at the water's edge. "Very well," replied the teacher, "but how will you get across the river? If you just jump on the raft you will be swept miles down stream and your raft may be crushed against the rocks." The heckler was full of impatience at such a silly diversion, replying that it was obvious that he would have also fashioned an oar to steer the raft across the river by his own power.

"Excellent," answered the teacher, "and when you get to the other side of the river, what will you do with your raft, my friend? Will you pick it up and carry it on your back in case you meet another river, or will you discard it and continue on your journey unburdened?"

The heckler looked scornfully at the teacher and replied that he would have to be mad to carry such a heavy burden with him just in case he happened upon another river. Of course he would discard it and continue unburdened.

"The same is true with my teachings and any others," replied the teacher. "Like the raft in the story, you will have to use your ***own energy*** *to* ***apply*** *the learning that will take you across the rivers in your life, however good your raft of learning might be, but*

when you reach your destination and the vehicle no longer suits your purpose, discard it and continue on your journey unburdened."

'Mind rafts' is a term I coined from this parable. It was originally taught to me by my friend and teacher, Bill Gould, the creator of a wonderful program of self-improvement called Transformational Thinking that we taught together for a number of years and has greatly influenced my thinking. It is a powerful metaphor for how people attach to their perception of reality supported by thoughts, ideas and values that they carry around inside their minds as if they will serve them forever. They will not. Learning is an endless task of adaptation and learning how to leave old ideas behind and continue with your life unburdened is the first step to revealing things about yourself that are simply impossible to reveal from within the limits of a perception that doesn't want to grow.

Despite being nothing more than conceptual vehicles that float you from one choice to another, mind rafts are also nothing less than the root of everything you will ever create in this world. If you choose to perceive your beliefs as transient and only as useful as the degree of contentment that they can create for you, then the adaptability that this brings to your mind will serve you forever as your expanding awareness slowly opens you up to possibilities that once seemed totally implausible. What you believe to be true or possible is a self-inflicted limit upon what you can achieve in your life but if your starting point is infinite potential this is a wonderful environment for your mind to explore. It helps to be flexible when you are journeying in an environment that revels in the volatility of constant change. You just never know when it might serve you to believe something different about the world than you did a few moments ago.

Conversely, if you choose to become stubborn and inflexible and be consumed by your ideas you will be doomed to repeat the same conditions that have shaped the suffering you and those around you have endured in your life thus far. This latter attitude personifies the inability to self-regulate that was so profoundly highlighted in Dr. Grossarth-Maticek's study. The fact of the matter is that the true value in any idea is measurable only by the distance it can take you on your personal journey though life. It has no other value than that. It is rare indeed that we demonstrate the daring to relinquish our grip upon an idea that has been a faithful servant to us because the common belief is that truth is absolute. Luckily, this chapter offers you the opportunity to begin divesting yourself of ideas that have become dead weight and the notion of truth is just the first one of them.

The Parable of the Raft leads us to a profound conclusion: truth is relative. It is personal. It is not absolute, or even if it were, it doesn't affect you or me one iota. All that matters in the creation of your personal reality is what you believe to be true. You are not creating a suspension bridge or a fine piece of machinery, so that kind of physical acumen can be left to the Institute of Weights and Measures. You are in the business of creating contentment and that is a philosophy of the heart and of feelings. The mind rafts you carry around in your head color every choice you make in life and it is irrelevant whether you can empirically prove their legitimacy or not. You will act upon them nonetheless and your reality will be colored in their image.

Inherent within the concept of a 'truth' is the unhelpful notion that once you have it, it stays that way forever. After all, nothing can be 'more true' than truth itself. We may all grow up in vastly different cultures, with different habits, philosophies, customs and experiences but we each cling to our own truth as if it is the only one that is true. This causes great schisms between people and nations because our inability to be more inclusive in our thinking is the root of all conflict. It is far easier to challenge the integrity of someone else's truth than it is for us to admit the inherent fallibility of our own.

One of the most profound learning points in all of nature is of transience; continuous change. This process refutes the very notion of truth, that there is anything ***absolute***. Everything is always in the process of becoming something else. Modern people are often obsessed with maintaining stability, employment, avoiding accidents and unforeseen events and generally trying to control or find ways around the natural process of change. It is just one more example of how we are out of kilter with the natural rhythms with which we were once entrained. However, if your purpose is spiritual self-improvement then recognizing that improvement and change are inseparable partners requires that you leave the beliefs behind that make the status quo attractive because your focus is now upon achieving different results in your life. Some of the best mind rafts you have ever learned will continue to be the invisible causes of the suffering from which you are seeking your liberation if you are not prepared to challenge what you think is right, true, desirable or sacrosanct. It is natural to outgrow ideas just as we might outgrow a pair of shoes. However good they might have been in the past, the only mind rafts that matter on a spiritual quest are those that reveal more of reality right here and now, not what it seems to be there and then.

Rather than seeking absolute truth, adopting a mind raft of subjective truth is now a better guide to achieving the peace you seek. The thousands of interconnected mind rafts in your head constitute your 'personal truth', a unique reality based upon how the world seems to you and you have to start getting them into step with where you are going in life. It is time to forget about the empirical and measurable reality of science for a few lifetimes and concentrate on what you can change in your personal reality right here and now. The foremost of these is what you believe reality to be. Developing an intimate understanding of your current perception of reality is essential if you want to adapt your personal truth to suit your spiritual purpose. Changing your future requires acceptance that your current truth is responsible for your present reality. In the world of mind rafts, right and wrong is irrelevant. You must ask yourself: "How does this mind raft serve me to get where I need to be as a spiritual being?" If it serves you, keep it. If it does not, discard it with thanks for bringing you this far.

The irony of all this is that 'personal truth' is something of a contradiction in terms until we can learn to use it as such. While yours should be totally unique, it is neither as personal as its name suggests nor as true as you might believe it to be. Where do your beliefs come from? Did you create them all yourself? Are you the free-thinking spirit you believe yourself to be? Probably not. Most of your mind rafts are bequeathed to you as a child, having passed through the millennia, across generations, from family to family, person to person and eventually embedding into your personal truth as the values by which you live your life. Every culture teaches its children what is right and what is wrong, what is good and what is bad, what we can do and what we cannot, how we should feel and how we should not, what we can say and what we must not, all regulated by the people who raise us. From our families to extended families, our teachers to our respected elders, our authority figures to our heroes, the difference between truth and deception is not defined by what is or is not real, it is defined for us by those people whom we most love and respect in this world. We bear this mind raft starter-kit forward into adulthood, carrying forth the flame of local traditions, customs and rituals to influence every family, neighborhood, province and nation to which we contribute the energy of our ideas.

The Tibetans say that by the age of seven a child has already been conditioned to their basic personal truth. When we have learned it from those we most love and trust in this world, is it any wonder that we are reluctant to challenge it? After just 2555 days of life our world-view is already die-cast and constituting the essential structure of every decision that will determine the quality of the next 24,000.

The product of shared mind rafts is the cultures and traditions that have shaped the diversity of nations in the world today. People naturally possess a strong instinctive urge to belong to a tribal belief system. We seek conformity within a group's beliefs and every group's beliefs have the same underlying premise: our group is best, our religion has the only true God, our truth is final etc. In other words, we all like to think we are right. We congregate around truth like moths to the flame, expressing it through our religions, politics and social status, to name but three. It fuels our sense of ego, of being a part of something tangible and real, which is a wonderful illusion to start with. It could be argued that the desire for support and connection to people through common beliefs is even stronger than the desire for us to actually believe them ourselves. When being right also means being isolated, most people will balk because isolation demands that you define who you are for yourself and that makes you a bigger target for the majority to snipe at.

There is a popular belief that people resist change simply because it removes us from our comfort zone. What we really resist is the threat change poses to the historical cord of belief connecting us to our families, friends and culture. Life is easier when we perceive the world in ways that also make sense to the people with whom we most closely associate. We fit in.

If you suddenly accept that some of your core mind rafts are no longer credible the different attitudes and behaviors you will adopt due to this may well alienate you from your parents, brothers and sisters, priests, monks or clerics, teachers and professors, nurses or healers, all those people who taught you who you were and still perceive you to be that person today. How many of us change our religion, for example? Not many. Even when we deliberately and directly contradict these learned beliefs, as rebellious young Westerners are prone to do, we still replicate the connection in some form. As Georg Christoph Lichtenberg, the 18th-century German scientist and satirist, said: *"To do just the opposite is also a form of imitation."* Although we might like to claim that we have freely creative minds, all ideas are second hand. Overcoming the social sigma and peer pressure to remain who other people want you to be is just one more challenge in the challenge of change.

This doesn't mean that your society's predominant mind rafts never change. There is adaptation in everything. Trends come and go; some are more obvious than others. For example, as modern societies across the world have slowly drifted away from rural life as farmers and taken to urbanization and factories, new mind rafts related to this change in habitat have arisen. Natural learning and patterns of people closely connected to the land have been superseded by mechanized thinking and linear logic in accordance with the ideas of the industrial revolution that still pervade modern ideology even today. This is an accelerating pattern in Asia, where I live, as the drift of minds away from the rural family unit (still essentially a tribal unit, I might point out) and towards urbanization is more pronounced than in Western countries that have been affected by it for a much longer period of history. Not only does awareness and sensitivity decrease as the natural mind becomes entrained with the structured artificial environments of modern cities, our beliefs about the world we live in adjust too, which is reflected in new thoughts, words and actions not always conducive to a better quality of life. This change in mind rafts is greatly responsible for the dramatic shift in values that has occurred in Asia in the last 30 years and the migration from the land to the city is unlikely to slow down. According to a study jointly published by the Asian Development Bank in December 2006, Asia's urban population is predicted to expand by 70 per cent to more than 2.6 billion over the next 25 years. As economic conurbations expand, family units contract. As material society expands, spiritual people contract.

Mind rafts are being replicated on a global scale. What is the inevitable result?

Suffering

In a few hundred thousand years of mental evolution you might imagine that someone would have come up with a sure-fire set of mind rafts for achieving total contentment, wouldn't you? Likewise, if someone had done so, it would not be unreasonable to expect the techniques to have become essential learning for everyone in the world today. Surely it would be so flawlessly effective at generating contentment that the internet would be awash with it, the front pages of every newspaper would have headlines lauding its name and every breakfast show from Andorra to Zanzibar would be interviewing experts in its practice.

Amazingly, the causes of suffering and the path to liberation from it ***are*** known and knowledge of this has been handed down for millennia. They are not a secret. They have been recorded through the ages in scriptures from the Vedas to the Bible. Total liberation from suffering ***is possible*** for anyone who chooses to wake up and do the work. So why do so few know anything about them, much less use them to achieve liberation? Because reduction of suffering is not the objective of society as a whole and therefore not part of the mind raft starter-kit handed to us at birth. The meditative practices, changes in lifestyle or expansion of beliefs that are necessary to wake up a mind schooled in conventional mind rafts, would differentiate us from the crowd and leave us exposed to the social marginalization we fear. It is a vicious cycle indeed that the suffering that bonds us to our neighbors also divides us from the joy that we so desperately seek.

The vast majority of people are not even aware of the painful cycles in which they have become ensnared and are therefore unable to seek alternatives. It is not difficult to understand why it is said that history repeats itself: the same ideas are cycling from adults to children, passed from generation to generation of people unaware of the causes of their suffering. It is time to stop this pattern by understanding the way modern values and behaviors exacerbate and feed a cycle of suffering and how we can end it simply by valuing different things.

Suffering is the result of two mind rafts that are endlessly repeated daily by billions who believe they will relieve their suffering. The first is the belief that pleasure reduces suffering. The second is that avoiding pain reduces suffering. These two mind rafts are called the spiral of desire and the spiral of aversion.

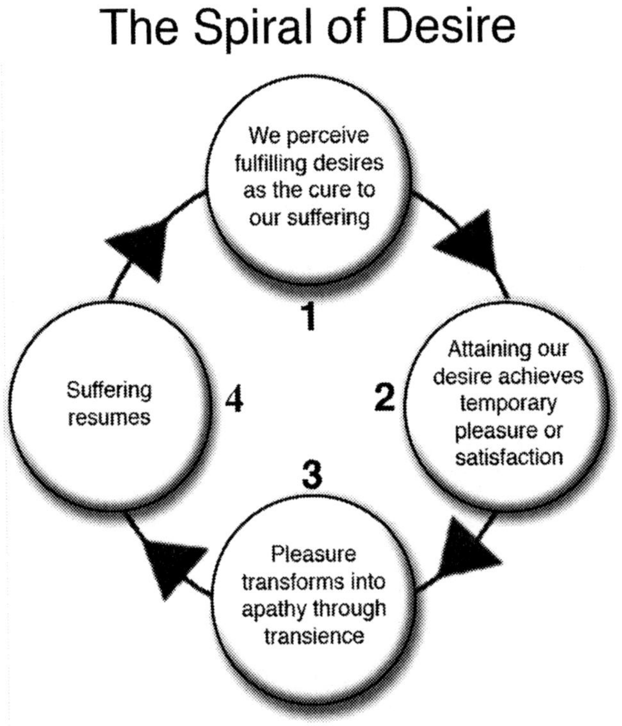

The Spiral of Aversion

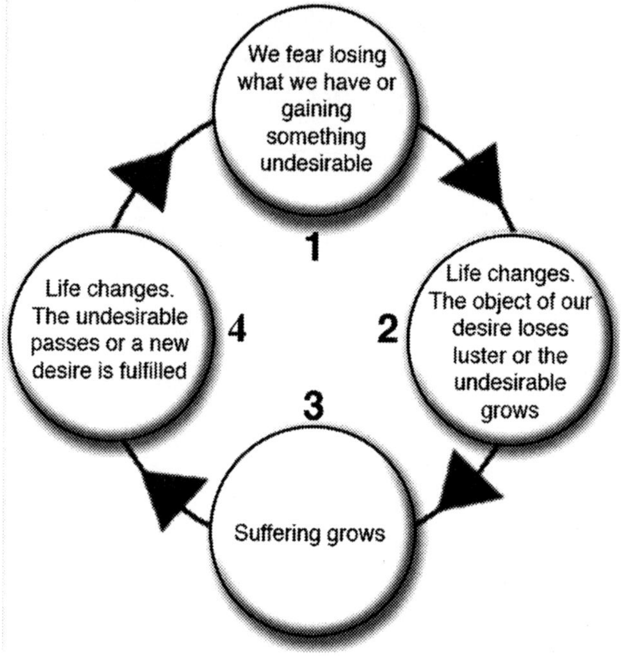

The spiral of desire sets us up for boundless disappointment and a need to keep feeding our desires because our feelings towards our subject change as we go through time. For example, if you desire a new car, once you have acquired it the beauty and allure of that car will one day fade as the car gets older and newer models are produced. What has changed most profoundly: the physical car or your mind's perception of it? Your attraction to the car wanes and your desire will eventually transform into suffering because the car will become old and ugly as your mind becomes bored with it. If your mind wasn't addicted to such a strange process, half of your suffering would be instantly extinguished. While the explanation makes it very clear to the reader that the mind is the cause of the suffering, not the car, most of us desire to change the car when the mind is a far better candidate for scrutiny.

The flip side of desire is aversion. We avoid anything that seems to contribute towards suffering or diminishes pleasure. While on one hand we seek pleasurable experiences, on the other we avoid anything that might upset us. This becomes apparent in our greatest fear, that of physical pain or death, which we avoid through the passionate acquisition of homely comforts, material possessions, life insurance and well-stocked refrigerators. It is an unfortunate byproduct of physical reality that the hardest, most painful and powerful moments of pain, emotional trauma and spiritual doubt are also those moments that offer the greatest potential for our transformation. Pain and suffering force us to adjust our path, to change, to adapt attitude and outlook, often transforming habits and behaviors that we would not independently adjust without such powerful physical motivation. As we will learn in later sections of Provolution, sickness is the body's way of screaming, "Wake up! Help! Change! Stop doing that!", or whatever it is you need to hear. So, although we may not welcome pain with open arms, it is neither healthy nor practical to focus so much of our energy on its avoidance. Modern culture runs in fear from these experiences because we believe them to add no value to existence when what we really lack is the sensitivity and awareness of what they mean and how to deal with them more productively.

Our adopted personal truth ensures recurrent suffering. The nature of the universe is one of transience and yet our approach to building contentment is struggling to maintain the consistent presence of objects and experience we like, while avoiding objects and experience that we don't. Yet desire always creates suffering and avoiding undesirable change is a physical impossibility, thus the mind rafts of desire and aversion have 100 per cent probability of ensuring more suffering in your life. As Dr. Grossarth-Maticek showed us in his self-regulation testing, being sensitive to the spiraling cycle of suffering and applying techniques to liberate yourself from it requires the divestment of mind rafts that may have adorned your personal truth ever since you were born. This is why it is a little tricky. But just as mind rafts have been learned, so they can be unlearned.

Freedom from Suffering

When asked to state, in as simple terms as possible, the essence of Zen Buddhist practice, the Master Suzuki Roshi said, "Everything changes." It is not coincidental that the essence of Zen is also the essential nature of nature, for so many of the practices that we consider to be spiritual are merely methods of returning the mind to its purest natural state: being one with the nature of nature.

Leaving behind beliefs that have become a burden to you is not an easy task but we should not take it too seriously either. Cultivating awareness is such a powerful response to our suffering that any action taken in awareness is beneficial to you. Unmindful action causes all complications in life for we blame others when the damage is all our own. In this chapter you have simply learned to take responsibility for what you think and what it creates. If the only achievement you accomplish in your lifetime is to assume this responsibility, you will have achieved a state of remarkable power to affect positive change in your world and the world of those around you and yet it will have been built upon a foundation of such awesome simplicity: everything changes. Life is no more complex than that.

The transient nature of reality is something we all know of but rarely sit and experience in awareness. This is the essential difference between raw knowledge and awareness in the present moment. The mind is a frantic thing that flits from one idea to the next in a series of associations that often have little or no logical reason to arise other than being next in line. To become the surgeon of your reality you need to take a scientific approach to yourself, testing and measuring the results of your applied beliefs in the laboratory of your life. Don't believe things just because some clever soul tells you it's true. Take the time to be aware of your thoughts, the way you say things and the results of your actions. Find an awareness practice with which you are comfortable and that allows you to experience the true nature of your mind and its means of limiting your potential for contentment. This process begins by accepting that we all take our personal truth for granted and repeat it over and over again, becoming increasingly frustrated at the disappointing, if somewhat inevitable, quality of results that return to us in life. Resolving to live your day in awareness offers you the opportunity to transform the unconscious mental states causing you to mechanically repeat mental, emotional and behavioral patterns that have become the roots of your personal suffering. This newfound potential is no small achievement either. It is everything you need to transform everything else.

There is a famous story of King Solomon who was stuck in the cycle of suffering, as are most people in the world today. Solomon decided that one of his ministers, Benaiah Ben Yehoyada, needed to feel a little humility and so he sent him on a quest to find a fictitious ring that when looked upon in a sad frame of mind would transform the mind into happiness but when looked upon in joy, would transform the mind into sadness. He gave his minister six months to find it.

After looking without success and with the deadline just a day away, in desperation Benaiah Ben Yehoyada asked one of the poor jewelers in Jerusalem if he had ever heard of this fabled ring. The jeweler took an ordinary gold ring and carved something into it. Taking the ring into his hand, Benaiah Ben Yehoyada looked upon the inscription and knew he had found what he had been looking for. On the day of the deadline , King Solomon asked him, with a mischievous smile, if he had found his quarry. He was shocked to learn that he had. As the ring was handed over to him, Solomon read it in awe. It stated in Hebrew: gimel, zayin, yud, which began the words 'Gam zeh ya'avor';

'This too shall pass."'

I do not believe any phrase I have ever lived has helped me more than this one. For good reason, Suzuki Roshi chose a similar one to explain the nature of Zen. If you are able to apply this simple phrase to your life and look at all events as being a passage to the next event, a profound change occurs in how you go about things. You realize that beginnings and endings are illusions too. While you wait for the next good thing to start and the current bad thing to end you miss everything in between where there is just as much potential for your awakening lying dormant and awaiting your awareness to expand to the point where you believe it exists. Nothing is ever wrong. Everything is just perfect. Acceptance of this premise personifies the art of changing yourself, not the world in which your 'self' changes.

What would happen if you lived your life in the expectation that 'This too shall pass'? The current reality is a result of clinging jealously to ideas, to concepts, to thoughts as 'me' and 'mine' but what if 'This too shall pass'? What if you created an entirely different mental environment where nothing was fixed, nothing was permanent and nothing was true? All those things that you are afraid of losing would disappear, wouldn't they? All those things that you are afraid of feeling would disappear. All those things that you have but do not want would disappear. All those things that you don't yet have but desire to have would also disappear. When something loses the power over you that it once had, it is as good as gone. You see, suffering too is an illusion that drives us to find a place where realization can occur and suffering can end. If we change the way we perceive the world around us, we change what we can realize. As fear and threat disappear, faith and possibility become real.

The nature of many minds is blunt and stony. Little soaks into them. They learn how to cease changing. A typical adult body is about 53 per cent water[1] but we are born around 70 per cent water.[2] As we get older the ratio of water to body mass decreases.

Perhaps this accounts for the increasing inflexibility of mind as it gets older. However, it may also be the physical reaction we have conditioned by choosing to stop being flexible like water and as absorbent as a sponge. When we become too tired to learn or think that we already know everything worth learning this is the point when we reach the limitations of knowledge. Merely ***knowing*** transience is not enough to bring about change. For any transformation to occur we must begin to ***live*** transience in our lives once again.

Every time I conduct a workshop I always ask people what it is they think they can learn. I can read in people's eyes those who have no potential to learn, not because they ***possess*** no potential but because they ***perceive*** no one to learn from. They have lost the perceptive quality that once greedily soaked up experience and have become stuck in a different place and a different time when they have decided to learn no more. They now fail to project their imagination beyond their current mindset into a world where different things happen to them and new potential exists. Who and what can teach us is a matter of whether we perceive anything we need to learn and anyone around us to learn from.

Another aspect of this is the student who simply learns information but fails to apply it to change their reality. This is called selective ignorance and I have met plenty of people who find it far easier to claim that "It doesn't work", or "I don't have time". There is always good reason for not doing what you do not want to do, but knowledge without application is useless and a shift in awareness brings with it an equivalent expansion of responsibility if real transformation is to set in. People who wait around for others to bring about the reality that they desire are not really seeking peace at all, they are seeking safety, but in doing so they place themselves in great peril. Were you to consciously adopt a life based upon transience, a whole gamut of freedom would magically appear before you. It was always there of course. You were not yet ready to see it. Non-attachment to ideas, non-commitment to your thinking and non-possession of beliefs are all incredible freedoms that transform the entire landscape of learning for yourself and the children we must all teach to do things better than we have done them. In this environment there is no right or wrong, just ideas that enhance contentment and ideas that don't. For many, this may sound wishy-washy and vague but inclusivity ***is*** vague. Minds that seek absolutes may find a lot of black and white truth out there but this type of mind carries with it the pitfall of being trapped in an illusion that, if not relinquished, will forever seek freedom in desire and aversion. On the other hand, the vague mind, the transient mind, the mind that experiences but does not become, this is a mind that disappears before truth becomes its master and exists for no longer than it takes for an evolution in consciousness to occur.

Chapter 3

Chaos and Faith

"Doubt is not a pleasant condition, but certainty is absurd."
François-Marie Arouet (Voltaire) French Writer, Essayist and Philosopher (1694–1778)

Global Mind Rafts

Globalization is creating something of a paradox. Global technologies are connecting people together while global philosophies are alienating entire cultures that feel bullied and oppressed by them. Intellectual property has become the opiate of the global economy and there is none more valuable than the mind rafts that define the basis of our economic, political and social systems. Once wars were fought for land and plunder, now ideological supremacy has become the ultimate purpose for it guarantees the same economic victory but without the political fallout of violent confrontation. Warmongering has become mind mongering; the creation of habits and beliefs, but it is no less enslaving and arguably no less brutal either. The world is in a philosophical battle to determine which mind rafts become the tribal norm and you are just one of its soldiers. What you think, what you say and what you do have never been more important.

It is worth keeping in mind that all new ideas are conceived in the mind of a single person somewhere on earth. If the idea becomes popular, the trend that emerges from it influences the purpose in our lives and the values by which we live. We have already established that mind rafts are handed down to us through time and across generations and so we now recognize how difficult it is to evolve away from these trends and into new belief streams that support an expansion of consciousness and not just wealth. In this chapter we are going to examine how mind rafts evolve from personal truth into physical products and systems that have global influence. Understanding the role you play in this chaotic process will lead you to a greater sense of the enormous responsibility you have for being truly aware of all aspects of your personal truth and to provolve away from mechanical beliefs towards a greater faith in the natural processes in which we all live.

Mind rafts are not the objective concepts that we may imagine them to be. Seemingly amorphous and intangible, they are actually ***alive***. They may not have a heart, a central nervous system or free will, but mind rafts are born, grow, mature and die in the same way as all natural entities in this world through a process of:

- Expansion by connection
- Contraction by disconnection

Just like life, ideas are born and die too. They expand and contract, ascending in popularity as people connect to them and apply the ideas to their life in some form, or declining in popularity if people reject them and choose other options. This process is the same for mental concepts, physical life or indeed entire realities. All things arise and fall by a mechanism of connection and disconnection whether built from ideas, molecules, bricks or words. There is very little difference in process between building a human being by connecting cells together in a womb and people building their reality by connecting mind rafts together to create personal truth.

As people around the world share an idea, practice habits built from that idea or buy products designed around it, the idea expands and flourishes just as life flourishes when more nutrients flow into a physical body. If you stop feeding a body it will break down and die in precisely the same way as if you stop feeding any idea or system with the energy of expansion. Just like physical beings, ideas that are not expanding will contract and eventually disappear altogether.

For three hundred years, the Western world has been investing its energy in expanding the ideas of the industrial revolution and it is time that we began realizing the great limitations these ideas bring to our personal minds and our shared reality. This epoch of huge social, political and economic transformation was enabled by iconoclastic concepts from luminaries like Newton, Boyle, Maxwell, and many other scientists who contributed a quantum leap in human knowledge through their science. If their ideas hadn't inspired the entrepreneurial spirit of inventors like Stephenson and Brunel, the world today would still look very much as it did then. Instead, the next 100 years saw the ideas of the industrial revolution expand like wildfire across Europe and eventually all across the world. Why? Because the ideas of the industrial revolution had a ***perceived advantage*** over the ideas that they superseded.

People choose to live by ideas and use products that they perceive offer them an advantage in achieving their goals in life. It is a form of natural selection powered by free will. If making money is your objective, you will choose ideas that are perceived to help you do so quicker, just as you will choose other ideas if spirituality is your goal. The idea of the selfish gene in genetics, that the strongest 'genetic mind raft' overcomes weaker genes, rings true for the survival of ideas and the resulting trends they create across the globe. While the strongest gene will be that which provides the life form with the best competitive advantage in its environment, people aren't always as sensitive to what constitutes an advantage because our free will is based upon the limits of perception.

We saw in Dr. Grossarth-Maticek's experiment in Germany that the key to adaptation is first being ***aware*** of a negative influence before you can choose to adapt behaviors to be more positive. If you are unaware of the negative downside of ideas that appear to have 'perceived advantages' in your reality, you will keep choosing them as preferred options in life. A drug addict must first perceive the damage the drugs are doing to him before he can choose to stop taking them. If being stoned all day is perceived as an advantage over being sober, quitting drugs will not seem a positive option, however much damage other people can see the drugs causing. Just as genes naturally and continuously select options according to external forces in their environment, people are equally influenced by these forces but are neither as sensitive to them nor as ready to react and choose something different. To change habits or behaviors people often need the force of sickness, depression or desperation before they choose to change. The question you face in this context is whether the perceived advantage of the mind rafts you have expanded in your reality thus far is really an advantage in your goal of provolution? Or are you simply unaware of the damage they are doing?

The revolutionaries of the industrial age weren't as aware of the power of mind rafts as the provolutionaries of this spiritual age will be. They did not know what results when we funnel human energy into expanding the disconnection of one person from another or in desensitizing people to the natural patterns of the world. The disadvantages of our preferred mind rafts are well concealed because our perception often sees only what we would prefer to choose. As an example of what I mean, let's take just one of the mind rafts that powered the whole epoch of the industrial revolution, Boyle's Laws, which describe the behavior of heat and pressure.

Boyle, like most men of his time, perceived the universe as a huge mechanical watch and God as the watchmaker. Therefore his laws for heat and pressure reflect the mind rafts of order and consistency that he saw in the world around him. When applied to the creation of the steam engine, however, Boyle's laws adopt a physical form that embellishes them with many other values, some of which we will perceive as great advantages and others which we will not even perceive at all because we are not looking for them.

What are the perceived advantages of the steam engine? Few of us would argue that convenience, speed and efficiency sound like very useful advantages but if this is all we see then our perception is missing the flip side of the coin. The values of a steam engine also encourage faster and greater consumption of natural resources to power it, an increase in air pollution, degradation of natural landscapes to run the rails, greater noise pollution etc. While it might sound logical to value convenience over inconvenience, efficiency over inefficiency and speed over slowness, the perceived advantage doesn't seem so clear cut when we also recognize we are valuing convenience over natural beauty, speed over pollution and time efficiency over accelerated consumption of natural resources. If we understand that advantage is a perception, we will recognize the fundamental importance of expanding awareness of our personal value set to identify whether it is a real advantage to us or just a convenient perception.

Your every creation in life occurs by applying mind rafts that expand one reality and contract another. Everything that you think, say and do has this effect. Your actions reflect the values that you believe in and also those you are prepared to sacrifice in order to gain your perceived advantage. In turn, you contribute to the global pool of habits that gradually entrain the world to those values. What one day may be shocking and controversial becomes commonplace the next. Normality is very difficult to evolve because our personal truth reinforces values in the shape of habits that we become loathed to adapt.

Just as at any other point in human history, today every physical product, political system, economic process, educational establishment, business unit or neighborhood is an accurate reflection of the values we perceive to bring us an advantage in the pursuit of our personal and collective goals, as well as being the antithesis of those that we don't. These values are wired into the mind of every man, woman and child who accepts them for what they are ***and*** what they are not. The global reality is as much constituted by our mind rafts as our mind rafts are influenced by the reality we create. It is a spiral of connected parts that feed each other, which is why it is so difficult to change the world and far easier to change your own.

The globalized world still clings to a great many of the mind rafts that powered the industrial revolution and technologically they have served us well. Sadly, we ignore the darker values inherent within them that have been responsible for environmental destruction and personal discontentment on a global scale. Just like the steam engine before it, every new technology that values speed, volume and convenience sacrifices other values more closely related to human contentment. Speed, volume and convenience just do not hit the spot. As we pour our energies into the pursuit of knowledge and technologies, we also contract the energy available for our development of quality human relationships and awareness. They are a different value set. This usurps the purpose of contentment and feeds the spiral of suffering as surely as if we were intending it. The amazing thing is, most people are completely oblivious of the part they play in it.

On the creation of the atomic bomb Albert Einstein said: *"The release of atomic energy has not created a new problem, it has merely made more urgent the necessity of solving an existing one."* This describes perfectly the current reality. In the same way that atomic weapons expanded human potential to destroy ourselves, so the expansion in technological connectivity expands our potential to spread and replicate the set of values that are responsible for the current reality. Our interconnected, interdependent communications systems, satellite network and World Wide Web facilitate the evolution of events at speeds that were literally unthinkable just 20 years ago. The dissemination of an idea emerging in Argentina is no longer hindered by village boundaries, trade routes, horse riding messengers or postal services. Ideas are instantaneously transferred to a global audience of bloggers and e-mailers, cable viewers and SMS messengers, Twitter broadcasters and Wikipedia readers. It is predicted that the 21st century will spawn a volume of change equivalent to that cumulatively experienced in the previous 60,000 years of human evolution. While this may herald exciting times for economic and business growth, it is a false prophet. The resulting volatility and magnitude of change augurs frequent catastrophic and unpredictable global events caused by people whose values are not based upon the interconnectivity and interdependence of our race but upon the perceived advantage of values that were born in the industrial revolution.

"There is more to life than increasing its speed," said Gandhi, but the trend towards acceleration is unlikely to contract unless we determine a more pressing objective. The depth of the 2008 global downturn, the suicidal consumption of natural resources, regular stock market crashes, oil price fluctuations, extinctions of flora and fauna, currency speculations and countless other results are just symptoms of how our current values expand the sharing of information but contract the sharing of relational values seeking human contentment. Though we now rely upon computers to be our sensual detectors for economic events, they are useless as sensors for our spirits. The good news is that all this connectivity offers the individual a far greater power to touch the world than in any previous age. If we can learn some different values that kindle the unlimited potential of people to value kindness, community, sharing and the need to stop and smell the roses on this journey of life, the values of the industrial revolution will contract and the mechanisms of the technological age will expand into connections of the spiritual age.

The Butterfly's Wing

It is not difficult to imagine how the action of one person pressing a button to send up nuclear warheads affects the reality of many other people; it goes without saying that dramatic actions can influence events around the globe via dramatic effects. However, ***you*** have an equally spectacular personal power to affect change all over the world. Subtle adjustments to your own behavior can create momentous effects in the lives of people around you and are multiplied and expanded by others committing themselves to the same habits and goals. In the same way that nothing conspicuous occurs when people randomly move around a small boat, if enough people move to the same side of the boat simultaneously, it may capsize. This is the power of synergy and our personal contribution to the chaos that is a key natural mechanism in how things change and why it is essential for people to take a greater responsibility for the change we contribute towards.

Surprisingly, chaos is not a new discovery. It has taken more than a century to begin entering the collective consciousness as a force to be reckoned with. It's identification was actually a somewhat chaotic in itself. In 1887, King Oscar II of Sweden offered a sizable monetary prize to the first person who could solve the three body problem. This was a problem that was known to exist in Newton's laws of gravity. While Newton's model worked fine when calculating how the gravity of two planets would interact, nobody could explain why the model didn't seem to work when a third planet interacted with the other two. Newton's model was based upon stability, for it was assumed that, were the universe unstable, the planets would have either collapsed into the sun or been thrown out into the coldness of the galaxy long ago.

Henri Poincaré, a French scientist, took up the challenge by using Newton's theories to create an orrery, a simple model of the universe, comprised of a sun in the middle and one planet orbiting it. In this model, Poincaré's calculations initially ran according to the established theory. The orrery performed as if the solar system was stuck in repetitive motion. Poincaré then added a comet to the orrery on an extremely elliptical orbit that swung all the way to the outer reaches of the solar system and then back in towards the sun, passing by the single planet's orbit as it did so. Running the calculations over extended periods of time, Poincaré initially failed to record any changes to the orbits as expected but then, during one calculation, the comet passed close by the planet and suddenly both the orbit of the comet changed and, much to Poincaré's surprise, the orbit of the planet also became slightly more elliptical. This alone was fairly earth-shattering news because it revealed the Newtonian fixed and stable model of the universe to be inaccurate. But there was more.

When Poincaré ran his calculations again, this time starting the comet in a slightly different orbit, he expected to get the same results, yet as he calculated the history of his imaginary solar system once more he was amazed to discover that over an extended period of time the entire history of his orrery turned out very differently indeed.

Poincaré won King Oscar II's prize. He had discovered that the universe was both unstable and that rule-based systems such as Newton's calculus and gravitational mechanics, previously considered the ultimate description of God's universe, could produce chaotic, unruly results. Science was beginning to realize that the accepted mind rafts of a predictable and consistent universe were not the only ideas on God's mind.

It was not until 1960 that the extent of Poincaré's discoveries would be revealed and expanded upon by some awesome revelations. Once again, it occurred through a chaotic process of assumptions and mistakes by the American meteorologist Edward Lorenz. He had set up his computer to run 12 different computational models of the weather in order to predict different sequences. At one point he wanted to run one of the models again, but rather than start the whole process from the beginning he chose to take the computer generated data and input a piece of code from the middle of the sequence. The printed code was good to three decimal places and so he entered the data to start the sequence as 0.506 when the actual data being used by the computer was based on six decimal points and read 0.506***127***. At the time, accepted mathematical reasoning assumed the difference between the two numbers to be so miniscule as to make no difference to the outcome but when Lorenz returned to his experiment an hour later he found incredible differences between the original results and the new ones. He had discovered what is commonly known today as 'the butterfly effect'. If a butterfly flaps its wings in Hong Kong, could it cause a twister in Kansas? This theory suggests that tiny causes can contribute to potentially huge effects over extended time periods. While Poincaré proved that chaos existed in even the most organized systems, Lorenz demonstrated the massive potential of each human being to affect change in any system at all.

I wonder how many people on earth today concur with Lorenz's original belief that small causes have little or no effect on reality? Yet natural chaos suggests that individual causes contribute to the collective reality like water dripping into a bucket drop by drop. It means that all causes are intimately connected to one another and that effects are a combination of all causes simultaneously conditioning each connected effect. Chaos rejects the limited degree of personal responsibility each of us prefers to assume for global events. We tell ourselves that we are not responsible for the destruction of the rainforest because we do not wield the axe. We claim to be immune from responsibility for war because we do not pull the trigger. We assume no responsibility for economic collapse because we do not control the banks but if we understand and recognize the dramatic potential of one butterfly's wings, we might confer upon our thoughts, words and actions the presumption of a greater power than we currently do. Chaos demonstrates that the collective reality is a product of ***everyone*** creating it, expanding it or contracting it and your personal values and mind rafts do affect global conditions. By discounting this influence, you expand your faith in separation and independence from other people, when nothing could be further from the truth. We are all connected.

Say you purchase a can of soda. You may not perceive this as being a major choice in life and you are certainly not intending to harm anybody but it has major chaotic ramifications if you look for them. You are not just investing in a beverage but in every value, intention, word and action that went into creating it. By purchasing the product you also buy into the people, systems and ideas that the product supports. Not only do you purchase the liquid and the aluminum can, you also buy into every aspect of the production process and connected activities. From mining the ore to shipping it, from the sugar plantations to the political systems in the countries growing the sugar cane, from the cost of the roads transporting the raw materials to the conditions in the factories processing it, from the families who take home a wage in the canning factory to the human resources policies of the management, from the water resources being extracted from the earth to the cleanliness of the processes filtering it, from the taxes levied on the exports to the expenditure of those taxes on weapons or education, from the intentions of the shareholders to the way in which they reinvest their profits; what extent are you willing to accept responsibility for the state of your reality? The interconnected and interdependent representation of nature that we are discussing here is a far better reflection of reality than the traditional perception that we barely affect one another at all. As heavy as this burden may be, it should not cause us to recoil in fear of action. Doing something or doing nothing contributes with equal energy anyway. It should cause us to rediscover what so many of us have lost: faith.

Faith

With stark clarity, chaos illustrates why it is so important that you change. Changing ***you*** is enough. It makes such a difference to all things. Sadly, so many of us are caught up in the industrial revolution mind rafts of control and predictability, order and structure that we think we can plan and organize our way out of the spiral of suffering. If it hasn't worked so far, perhaps you need to try something a little different. Faith is a great place to start.

Faith is often used in a religious context but let's adjust its meaning for the benefit of provolution. Faith is choosing on gut feeling. It is accepting chaos. It is living with the fact that you can never really predict with certainty the outcome of your choices. It is realizing that you are not in control of what happens but you are in control of what you do and how you feel about it. This may seem an unnecessary burden to minds schooled in the intellectual superiority of logic but it is an obligation to those dedicated to expanding spirituality. Any choice made in a chaotic environment will ultimately be made on faith… and planet earth is certainly a chaotic environment.

It seems to me that Western society has spent the last few thousand years dissecting the earth in order to control it and become its master in the belief that surrendering to universal will is a defeat of some sort. We have run afraid from nature's dark places, divided ourselves from its patterns, and from this state of detached unawareness projected a fearful belief that unless we control nature we will forever be at its mercy. This is surely a projection of ego. In chaos we learn that most human struggle for control is futile. Rather than reducing suffering, it deepens it and is therefore wholly self-defeating. Thomas Merton, the American writer and Trappist Monk said: *"The truth that many people never understand, until it is too late, is that the more you try to avoid suffering the more you suffer because smaller and more insignificant things begin to torture you in proportion to your fear of being hurt."*

How truly this is reflected in our fear of nature and our rejection of faith. The more we try to control it, the less faith we have and the greater the spiral of suffering that we are compelled to repeat and augment.

Throughout this first part of Provolution you are piecing together how your left-brain has wrenched control of your life from your whole being. Right now, it is time to make a few hard choices and understand their implications in how you live. Thus far, you may have found it easy to accept that awareness and sensitivity are more useful to you than pure knowledge. That makes sense to the vast majority of people. It is even relatively easy to accept that your life has been fashioned from mind rafts passed through your society and that change in the world begins by creating it inside your own self. That is fairly logical too. It does not even stretch the imagination too far to envisage that chaos is a serious, powerful, natural mechanism that renders every choice you make a lottery dependent upon the fluttering of billions upon billions of tiny wings across the world. If science says it is true, it must be, right? But none of these realizations matter a jot if you are not willing to ***apply*** what all this implies. Chaos implies developing faith in the conditions that the universe organizes around you. It says that you do not have control of all these conditions. It implies that you will ***never*** have control and that most control is an illusion. Ironically, it also demands you accept yourself as the creator of the illusion.

You have arrived at the point in Provolution where you need to make the choice between expanding more control and expanding a little more faith. The mind rafts of the industrial revolution still haunt people's desire to manufacture a predictable life of plans, budgets and security from threat. We have become encumbered by a three hundred-year-old trend in personal truth that reinforces our sense of impotence to produce change on a monumental scale because our physical body cannot lift a ton weight or run for 48 hours without a break. Thus we apply this perceived limitation to spiritual, emotional or philosophical problems. By placing our faith in muscle power, we have abandoned the power of faith that once moved mountains and would do again if we could once more feel its limitless potential lying dormant within our hearts.

If faith has become difficult for you to generate, this is because you have spent your life listening to just one half of who you think you are, tuning in to the left brain and giving it a damn good work out while allowing the right brain to wither just as the muscle of an unused limb might atrophy. If you had spent your entire life listening to only one tune on a radio, you might believe it was the only tune ever written. We are all tuned in to logical left-brain thinking because all around us is blaring the same left-brain tune through economics, engineering, politics, the military, law, education, etc. Everywhere you look, you see the left-brain staring back at you!

Your left brain is the half of you that generates your strength of conviction, it strives to be accurate, precise and definitive, and its strengths lie in its power to discriminate, think in sequential steps and to break things down into parts and pieces. It is the part of you that follows sequences and loves planning. While it does not reject faith, it supplies the objective alternative, increasing the odds of your survival through analysis and reason. Although I may have been a little critical of left-brain thinking, it is also essential to your existence. Building a safe bridge needs left-brain engineering, operating on a heart needs left-brain technology, going to Mars needs a jolly good left-brained plan, but these are not the only human activities in life. Spiritual provolution needs a different brain.

The right brain is the seat of creative and emotional thought. It loves to see the bigger picture, to imagine, to envision, to make creative leaps of faith, to play with ideas and be intuitive. It is flexible and open, sees patterns and shapes in all things and is able to empathize and feel. The physical world that built the human brain is clearly telling us that there are two ways of perceiving reality and both of them are necessary and complimentary. Unfortunately, we often see these two different perceptions as being mutually exclusive. Yes, there are parts and pieces in this world that we can classify, organize and categorize, but these are connected to a greater whole. Without the right-brain ability to see the entire universe and all its connections together at the same time, how do we place this universe in context except in faith that the context is our own perception?

Left-brained thinking processes like logic are the primary means of perceiving the world in our globalized society. This is what we call the 'male' brain. We have learned that a good, logical brain will help us succeed in education and in business and therefore secure our economic future. It is responsible for our predominant social hierarchy and provides our sense of values and morality based upon rational thought. It believes in one right way and infinite wrong ways. It cannot accept two opposing ideas as being equally right. It is not difficult to imagine how such an exclusive thinking process might subjugate and marginalize a softer, more inclusive 'female' thinking system, and this is exactly why females are often dominated and oppressed in our male-centered world.

The problem with this intellectual approach to life is that it only listens to half the story being expressed by your own physical form and ignores the rest. If you use only left-brain logic to define your world, parts and pieces is all you will see and the first part you will see is yourself. If you take a spark plug, a steering wheel and a brake, you will have three things that individually spark, steer and decelerate, but if you join them together with other things, you have a car. Each person easily identifies their personal individuality, whether they are a spark plug, a steering wheel or a brake, but does not see the connection to the car of which they are a tiny but significant part. We are unable to connect to a bigger picture because we do not have faith that something we cannot see or touch can also exist and if we do not have faith that it exists, we will never start looking for it. This mind raft ultimately leaves people vulnerable and alone, not strong and resilient, as left-brain thinking would have us believe. While the left brain of logic perceives individual people and loves classifying them as talented, ugly, clever, beautiful, charming or aggressive, few people are able to see the entire species of humanity for the awesome collective it really is or the way our species connects with other species, the planet and the universe as a whole. If we did, war would cease and the fight for compassion would begin in earnest.

Generating faith in a chaotic world means accepting that you can never know the greater picture to which you contribute, for the ripples that you make in the ocean of life spread far beyond your sensual ability to detect them. Regardless of this, there are natural processes in life in which you can place your faith knowing full well what the results will be. They are obvious. If you live your life expressing love, gratitude, hope, joy and inspiration to those around you, these ripples extend far beyond those who would hear it, feel it or see it directly. Just imagine the energy you would be expanding and the mind rafts you would be supporting and you will know what I mean. You might personally feel a mere drop of the change you would affect on this planet but by the laws of chaos you would know that the results of your choices stretch out further and last longer than you can possibly imagine.

Embracing faith and accepting the power of the non-tangible world is an incredibly powerful statement of intention that has profound implications for how you behave. For one, it means that you do have purpose in life, although you may not know what it is yet. It also means being who you are without fear that it is wrong or feeling threatened by the majority who do not like you to be different from them. Faith gives rise to courage and courage to the passion that engenders the resolve to explore potential that you must believe you already possess before you will ever see it. Faith says believe it and you will see it, where logic says the opposite.

In faith you can keep going when times are tough and believe with all your heart that things will get better, which they will. This too shall pass. It gives you the power to overcome barriers telling you that you can't achieve your dreams and fills you with the certainty to know that you undoubtedly can. At the same time it inspires those around you to become all they can be because they see in your heart the faith that no one has ever become everything they can become. One inspires another, two inspire four, four expands to eight and in the spirit of this enlightened view of others' faith evolves a belief in people, in potential and in the infinite ability of everything to improve however bad things get.

Faith gives you a power that proof never could. It is the key to an endless resource of potential that would never exist for you if you did not believe it was there. In faith you know that what will be will be and that everything that happens is just another ripple of chaos to which we are all connected and all responsible. For faith is surrendering your personal will to natural mechanisms that human minds and hands will never control and by these means we escape the rigidity of thought that renders us hard and unyielding. It fills people with a power that liberates us from the illusory sense of success and failure empowering our suffering in repetitive cycles.

I am not suggesting you live a life that throws caution entirely to the wind but that you merely strike a finer balance between the fear of risk inherent within everyday tasks like crossing the road or driving to work and the greater risk of being so wary that you fail to embark upon undertakings that fill you with the spirit of adventure while doffing your hat to life's grand scale. Do not delay action on your dreams, your life's aspirations and your desire to be spiritual, the boldest tasks that inspire fear but portend joy, while you await the absolute certainty that your endeavors will be successful. It will not appear. It cannot. You must have faith that success is not the end of the journey at all. It occurs on the path, on the job, during the process of life, not at its end, in both pain and glory, but a failure to even step foot on the path reduces the majesty of life's journey to a series of minor hops from one safe rock to the next learning little, risking less. A discovery of your own self, your own peace, your own spirituality is ***not*** a risk, although it appears the greatest you have ever entertained, for you must leave behind the safety and sanctity of control that has guarded you against the rigors of transformation for so long and place your future in the hands of a guardian you do not yet know. Do not be afraid. You cannot be broken. According to the Roman scholar Marcus Terentius Varro: *"The longest part of the journey is said to be the passing of the gate."*

You can embrace chaos and plunge into a reality where you are a leaf on an ocean of time or seek to educate yourself to the point where you believe that no possibility could escape your intellectual grasp. One of these options accepts the universe for what it is. The other demands it become what you might wish it to be. If you can embrace chaos and change as constant companions, you expand faith that wherever you end up, it is where you are meant to be. You arrive at a point where universal interconnectivity and interdependence reveals chaos as nothing more than your inability to make connections between infinitely complex causes and effects and soon suffering falls away for you cannot suffer when you know, without qualification, without a shadow of a doubt, in absolute faith, that you are right where you need to be to learn all that you need to learn. If the universe really extends into infinity, then seeking infinite causes to infinite possible outcomes is a task only the ego of intellect could undertake. The spirit, on the other hand, would accept chaos on faith and begin to trust in the ultimate elegance of a life lived entirely by accident.

Chapter 4

Interconnection and Interdependence

"The goal of life is living in agreement with nature."
Zeno of Citium – Greek Philosopher (334 BC-262 BC)

A Universe of Parts and Pieces

If everything in the universe were independent from everything else, nothing would change. Nothing could relate to or affect change in anything else. There would be no chaos. There would be no interaction. In fact, there would be nothing at all. If the universe were made in truly separate parts every 'part' of the universe would live in its own isolated box and be impotent to affect change in anything around it. You could not affect anything else either because you would not even be aware that it existed. This is the picture of an independent, disconnected universe but this isn't the universe in which we live, is it? Well, if commonly applied mind rafts were anything to go by, you would be forgiven for believing that it was.

So much of our intellectual endeavor is based upon cutting up the world into measurable, manageable parts that it seems as if we are disinterested in doing much else. Indeed, those of us who seek to put it all back together into a more complete picture are often ridiculed for suggesting that objective parts could have anything so abstract as meaning. Thus, biologists categorize nature, time is chopped into pieces by archeologists and geologists, atoms are cut up into parts by physicists and doctors divide one organ from the next. Conventional providers of our truth separate everything into parts and pieces as if it that is the only way things could be. But is that really the case? Let's look at how the mind rafts of separation and independence have been passed down from one epoch to the next and why its universal application are primary contributors to conflict and suffering.

2500 years ago, the Greek philosophers Leucippus and Democritus speculated that all change in the world was a result of interplay between 'atomos', which literally translates as meaning something ***indivisible.*** This is how the concept of atoms first emerged. Indivisibility implies that something can't break down, can't change, can't evolve; the particle that they envisaged would stand throughout time as the immutable cornerstone upon which all physical matter was built. The Greeks, founding their personal truth upon an ordered pantheon of Gods, had a vested interest in maintaining this belief. Chaos challenged the very idea that Gods could control or predict anything. Thus, the atomic particle was a natural product of Greek thinking. As with all mind rafts, it had a perceived advantage. It didn't necessarily need to be true.

Plato has the dubious distinction of popularizing the idea of eternal forms and won the battle with Aristotelian thinking when his theories were revived during the European Renaissance. The great scientific thinkers that would become the founding fathers of modern science, Galileo, Copernicus, Kepler etc. held to the view that the mathematical truths they were deciphering were Platonic in substance (unchanging) and Christian in outlook (immaculate). Quite literally, they believed they were the describing ideas that had been born from the unadulterated mind of God, rendering Him the ultimate mathematician, an idea that endures even until today.

For over 2000 years, the immutable atom concept persisted and scientists like the Russian Mendeleev would give great credence to the concept with such revolutionary work as his Periodic Table. However, modern physicists now know that protons, neutrons, pions and all sorts of other sub-atomic particles exist within the atom, demonstrating them to be a product of many smaller parts. No immutable part has even been found and, as we will learn, none is ever likely to be found. Chaos and probability have been demonstrated to be physical laws that exist alongside Newton's gravity, Einstein's relativity or any of the other deterministic laws.

Despite all this, the mind raft of separation endures because we are neither schooled in the science of how one aspect of the universe connects to the next, nor, I highly suspect, desire to learn of it with any more zeal than the ancient Greeks. Much of what we believe about our selves, our personal possessions, our rights, our independence etc., requires a mind raft of separation for it to be plausible. It is much less convenient to adopt responsibility for the lives of other people around us. Our separation and focus upon the pleasures of independence divorces us from the way the universe is and confines us all to the tiny box of the way it seems.

Local and Universal Interdependence

In a room there is a carpet, a table and a chair. The chair ***seems*** separate from the table, the table ***seems*** separate from the carpet, the carpet ***seems*** separate from the floor etc. but this is merely an illusion of physical reality that you have accepted as true. The connections between all things enable the chair to knock up against the table, the table to imprint into the carpet and the carpet to push upwards with a force that supports the weight of the table. Nothing can change alone. Things are both separate ***and*** connected. Change is a relationship between different connected parts affecting one another. This means that all objects can, must and do interact with one another for any change to occur and they interact because they are connected together as ***one***.

While the chair, the table, the carpet and the floor appear to be fixed objects, this is an illusion perpetuated by our notion of time. Imagine what will have happened in a thousand years when their shapes will have broken down, the connected elements fallen away and each will have contracted into dust. Their elements can then connect with and expand into other things, recycling into the universal resource of energies, never dying or disappearing; just transforming. Without interdependence, this could not happen. If things were truly separate, how could they constantly expand and contract in evolving relationships with one another? In a thousand years the carpet could become a table, the table could become a chair and the chair could become a carpet. But interdependence implies even more than this…

Interdependence isn't only a local issue. It is a universal phenomenon. True interdependence does not just refer to objects in physical proximity to one another, such as the chair next to the table but the interdependence of everything in the universe, wherever it may be located. It implies a connection between all things, at all points and at all times. In other words, when you move the chair from under the table here on earth, ***the whole universe changes***. Seems pretty crazy, huh? These things normally do when core personal truth is being challenged.

For millennia Western thinking has sought to explain the universe as if it was a machine made from parts and pieces yet the subtle layers of reality have consistently bubbled up to confuse enquiring minds peering deeper and deeper into their depths. Around 1927 Niels Bohr and Werner Heisenberg peered deeper than anyone had ever peered before, penning 'The Copenhagen Interpretation of Quantum Mechanics', a groundbreaking, novel answer to one of the most enigmatic questions in physics: *'What is light made from?'* The answer would forever transform science because Bohr and Heisenberg were really asking whether one thing could actually be two things at once! It may sound a little absurd to even ask such a question: 'How on earth can one thing be two things?' It defies logic. This is where the right brain needs to come into play. Bohr and Heisenberg were asking a totally paradoxical question from a left-brain perspective but, when placed in the context of interconnectivity, independence and the paradoxical nature of the universe, profound answers could result from the most implausible of questions. Bohr himself once said: *"The opposite of a correct statement is a false statement. But the opposite of a profound truth may well be another profound truth."* Bohr and Heisenberg were about to discover a truth of such profundity that they would answer one of humanity's most hotly debated questions while simultaneously opening a Pandora's Box of new ones.

For centuries before Bohr and Heisenberg, scientists had argued whether light was made of physical material or whether it was a wave, like sound, which has no physical dimensions. In the Copenhagen Interpretation of Quantum Physics, Bohr and Heisenberg predicted that a light wave contained the ***potential*** to transform into physical mass in the form of a photon particle. In other words, light had dual properties; it was two things! This revelation alone threw the scientific community into a frenzy but there was more to come. The two scientists also threw the nuclear bomb of all nuclear bombs into the cauldron of debate regarding the extent of universal interconnectivity and interdependence.

Bohr and Heisenberg further theorized that the force triggering the incredible transformation from a wave into a physical photon was conscious ***observation***. In a stunning break from convention they proposed that consciousness is a physical force, possessing the power to convert potential into actuality simply by its existence. Like salt being added to water and creating salty water, so consciousness added to any space has a transformative effect upon all that it experiences. This means that you, as a conscious observer, are the bridge connecting together probability with actuality; what is with what could be.

Look at it like this: a beach ball sitting on the sand has shape, size and location because it is physical. However, if that beach ball had somehow been created but had never been consciously observed before it arrived on the beach, all that would exist would be a wave of pure potential, spread out across the universe, awaiting realization. If you were to walk along that beach and perceive the ball with your consciousness for the first time, the wave would 'collapse' from probability and the potential within it would be released in the shape of the beach ball. It would ***appear*** simply because you looked at it. Einstein scoffed at this idea proclaiming: *"I like to think that the moon is there even if I am not looking at it."*

Interestingly, subsequent thought experiments like Schrödinger's Cat in 1935 seemed to prove both the Copenhagen Interpretation ***and*** Einstein right. Schrödinger postulated that matter, once appeared, could not change back into potential. Once something had 'chosen' to appear in the physical reality, it became a part of it and was subject to its physical laws. In other words, the moon really is there today; but it was consciousness that realized it and first brought it into being.

Your conscious participation in life is bringing to fruition the potential and the connected events that have been conditioned into the universe from the beginning of time itself. If we work from the (rather dubious) concept of the big bang, this gargantuan act of energetic creation would have spread waves of potential across the universe in equal parts, conditioning events that are unfolding now. This wave of potential ties one side of the universe together with another, one galaxy with the next, each particle with every other particle like a massive pool of energy from which all physicality becomes realized. If everything was once unified before the big bang, why do we assume that it isn't still? Only the mind rafts of separation and independence perpetuate the illusion that the universe is divided and it is the most powerful illusion humanity has ever perpetrated.

In 1998 a strange but profound answer to how this process works bubbled up from the quantum soup. In an experiment conducted in Geneva, Switzerland, by a team led by Nicholas

Gisan, it was calculated that, somehow, light photons could almost instantaneously communicate across a distance of over six miles in the same time that light could theoretically travel just three and a half inches. Traditional Newtonian physics cannot explain this result but the peculiar interconnectivity and interdependence proposed by Bohr and Heisenberg can. While we look at physical reality in straight lines by measuring the linear distance between two points, perhaps the connections between photons occur in a different dimension of space and time where space is shaped differently. Or perhaps there is a super-fast dimension of time/space that, through the act of conscious observation, slows the energy to the vibration of the physical realm, creating the appearance of coming into being.

While we may view our world in simple physical terms, experiments like Gisan's show that connections exist that are astonishing, imponderable and, by traditional left-brain measurements, simply impossible! We are learning that, at the sub-atomic scale, everything is connected, interconnected and able to interact over huge distances without any perceptible barrier. The impossible becomes possible but we must remember that the impossibility only exists because of the walls of theory that we have built around the infinite possibilities available to an open mind. People get dazzled by and addicted to the gross physical sheen of life but the universe is a deeper, subtler place whose nuances are discernible only if you are prepared to peel away the outer skin and study the details. The same is true of our dualistic thinking: black/white, truth/lie, right/wrong etc. This exclusive mindset reduces the elaborate and subtle nuances of the universe to crude shadows.

The mind rafts of permanence and disconnection vein our personal truth and define our perception of ourselves and the universe from which we desire to be separate and divisible because it suits our version of events. If we embraced interconnectivity and interdependence, every other mind raft would crumble like a house of cards. We would have to transform how we relate to our own self and the world outside of us or suffer conscious hypocrisy. Yet, we cannot create a new reality of less suffering without first creating a 'me' who suffers less, for one is inevitably a mirror of the other. As we now know, when we change our own self, the whole universe instantly changes with us.

Our Desire to Separate

It is important to understand that the mind rafts of separation and permanence are connected in the same way that interconnectivity and change are connected. You cannot accept one without the other because they are two halves of the same thing, like yin-yang. If you believe the world to be divided into parts and pieces, whether you know it or not, you will also believe that there is something permanent within those parts, a permanent existence that is self-sustaining. This mind raft enables your mind to discriminate between one thing and the next without having to answer the paradox of how something that is clearly impermanent can also be separate from what it is transforming into. Can a raindrop be called separate from the cloud? Can a sea be called separate from the humidity in the atmosphere? As we learned in the chapter on expansion and contraction, all things break down and form other things so they cannot really be separate at all. What we actually perceive in our minds is only the state of an object in the present moment of time. It appears more connected to one thing than another but that does not mean it is entirely disconnected from everything else. All we need do is wait long enough to observe it transform into another thing entirely.

You may look at your own body and conclude that your heart and lungs are separate parts but you also know they are a part of the same thing: your body. Your body may appear separate from the wind but one day your body will die, break down and become dust scattered by that wind. It is impossible to differentiate between 'two parts interacting' and 'two parts of the same thing'. Who decides what is what and where one things starts and another ends? Custom may define it. Prejudice may define it. Our mind rafts may define it. But there is no profound truth in the matter. Our preference to believe in separation creates a world of parts and pieces rather than unity and interconnectivity. It is a simple choice. But its implications in our lives are simply enormous.

If you accept for a moment that the rock and the sea are different parts of a unified whole, this is indeed a huge philosophical step. It demonstrates acceptance that two objects have a commonly intertwined present and future and that the direction of change in one of them is dependent upon and related to the direction of change in the other. Still, there is a greater leap of acceptance ahead of you. If you are to generate true peace and quality of life for yourself, you need to apply these mind rafts to more emotive relationships than those between apparently inanimate objects. Bringing the mind rafts closer to home, what does interconnectivity and interdependence imply regarding your relationship with your neighbor, the beggar on the street and Bill Gates, the President of the USA and Osama bin Laden, Jews to Muslims, pro-abortionists to anti-abortionists, the soldier to the enemy he kills, communists to capitalists? How does this affect your opinion on these relationships if you consider each and every one of them connected, dependent and reliant on one another too?

Acceptance of this degree of connectivity is profoundly difficult because our left-brain thinking has set us up to conflict with other people who seem to threaten us. Our minds are exclusive, not inclusive. When we become emotionally involved in powerful events, this exclusivity becomes extreme causing the energetic connections between our adversaries and ourselves to appear non-existent. In order to commit ourselves, our community or our nation to paths that would normally be abhorrent to us, we must first disconnect, dehumanize and divide people and issues into exclusive values like right and wrong, good vs. evil, law abiders against criminals. Divisive logic takes over and right-brain connectivity is ignored. How can Al Qaeda and Western culture be mutually dependent upon one another to exist, for example? How can Israel and Hamas be interdependent? How can stock markets and global poverty be interconnected? To the vast majority of people, these very ideas seem perverse, extreme, even blasphemous, when recognizing interdependence in opposing forces is really no more extreme than perceiving rain and the grass as being interdependent. You cannot pick and choose the application of a naturally occurring and objective universal force although we frequently do in order to fit in with our inconsistent application of values and beliefs.

You have trained your mind to be judgmental and categorical. Thus the world of black and white divisions, of right and wrong, of good and evil, soothes your mental needs. The intellectual pursuit of absolute truth requires watertight mental armor through which none of the confusing ambiguities of grey might seep. As science has enquired deeper beneath the superficial skin of the physical reality, ordinary people have failed to adapt our behaviors to include the new discoveries. Yet they are only new discoveries in scientific terms and would have been nothing more than common natural sense from the point of view of our nomadic ancestors. Modern people pick and choose our truth in order to maintain a paradigm that justifies the madness in our lives. To choose a different truth, a natural option, would require us to change everything that separates and divides us from one another. Rather than enquiring into why conflicts escalate and repeat themselves and by way of reply assume responsibility for the broken connections we have sown in the chaos, we neglect this responsibility by accusing others of hating our culture, of attacking our way of life, of insulting our gods or making victims and martyrs of our ancestors. None of this solves the problems. It deepens our inability to connect with and trust other people. Yet interdependence and interconnectivity teaches us that things are connected together to such an extent that we are really one thing, separated only by the walls around our ideas and fear within our hearts. Acceptance of your connection with every particle of energy and matter draws you into a partnership with life in which walls crumble, relationships expand, cooperation becomes beneficial and competition rendered ultimately futile.

All connections begin with you.

Chapter 5

I-go

"You must be the change you want to see in the world."
'Mahatma' Mohandas K. Gandhi (1869 - 1948) - Indian Statesman and Spiritual Leader

What is I-Go?

'Who am I?' is the ultimate question in life. The answer you give to this timeless quandary couldn't be more significant in determining why you choose the reality you do. Twenty thousand years ago, our nomadic ancestors answered the question by becoming one with the natural environment, generating sensitivity to it and awareness of their interconnectivity and interdependence. Two hundred years ago people had learned to answer it through the mind rafts of Newtonian physics that taught constancy, control and the division of one thing and one person from another. A century later and quantum physics had rediscovered the profound truth that had been a natural product of the nomadic lifestyle: the universe really is interdependent, chaotic and probabilistic and human consciousness interacts and affects the environment in the present moment. Today, few people apply these provolutionary ideas to their life or understanding of who they really are. Why not?

In this section we are going to answer the question 'Who am I?' by examining what is usually called 'ego'. However, we are going to develop a different mind raft than the conventional idea of selfhood by looking at the identity we build around ourselves in three layers: i-go, u-go and we-go. I-go is your self-perception, u-go is your perception of other people and we-go is the tribal culture resulting from an aggregate of all i-go's mixed together.

We will look at u-go and we-go in Part II of Provolution but for now, what is i-go and how does it dominate your reality?

I-go is the ultimate illusion of separation on a personal level. It says 'I' exist. 'I' am here. 'This' belongs to 'me' and 'these things' are 'mine'. It is every mind raft you possess about yourself. Humanity shares a common belief that something permanent and individual exists within each of us, an essence of who we are, a soul, a part of us that is unreservedly 'me'. Whatever we wish to call it, this is the same divisive sensation that precipitated the concept that atoms are the fundamental particle and the parts and pieces theory of the universe... but what is this part within us? Where does it begin and end? For millennia science has sought the static particle in the universe without success so can we really hope to find such a part within the human being? And if it doesn't exist, what does it imply that you journey through your whole life in separation from the world around you, believing that it does?

You may think you are your body, but which part of your body is really 'you'? If your whole body is you, then what happens if you lose a finger or a leg? Are you no longer 'you'? Even if your body is you, what about the hair or skin that falls away to be replaced by other bits of 'you'? When does dead skin stop being 'you'? How can you retain a constant impression of yourself when the air you breathe is changing, your blood is circulating and your body entirely regenerates every cell numerous times over the course of your life? How can a permanent 'you' always be changing?

Maybe your mind is 'you' or creates the perception of 'you', but your mind could not exist without a brain with which to know 'you' exist or without the rest of your body with which to support its existence. Your mind is dependent upon your physicality. But perhaps 'you' are what you know about the world, all your experience or knowledge? But your experience and knowledge are as transient as the ocean. They are never the same from moment to moment. The permanent essence of who you think you are changes and can never be captured as the single permanent thing you believe 'you' to be.

Perhaps 'you' are your soul but without a body or a mind 'you' would be very different to the 'you' whose body and mind experiences this world. If 'you' are a spirit or a soul what part does your mind and body play in your existence? Without them, how would 'you' feel any of what 'you' attribute as 'my feelings'? If they are not really a part of you, why do 'you' worry about them so much? Without a body and mind how could 'you' be aware of your own existence at all?

Why do we act as if a separate or static 'me' exists when there is no evidence of it? Although it may ***feel*** like 'I' exist, how many of us have really taken the time to check what 'I' really am? Even cursory consideration of the human condition reveals the same transient nature present within people as exists in everything else on this earth. There is nothing permanent to call 'me', so where does this sense of 'me' or 'mine' come from?

My wife and I had the great fortune to be blessed by the birth of our first child, Jacob, in early 2008. I quickly learned that children are not, as commonly believed, born pure and innocent. They are born full of i-go demanding 'my milk' screaming for 'I' to be attended to and very quickly learning to associate with the shapes and sounds of people who soon become 'mine'. In his first year and a half of life I witnessed his growth from one i-go phase to the next, constantly developing his needs, expectations and emotional range. I also experienced him conditioning the spiral of suffering in his reality by flitting from one toy to another, sensual experience to sensual experience, constantly seeking to extend the fix of fun that held his short attention span.

From watching our children grow up, adults learn the roots of their own i-go first hand. It is a survival tool present from birth. Initially it demands safety, warmth and nutrition but quickly develops sensual desires and aversions angling for a permanent state of fun. Like any tool, any mind raft, i-go will serve my son when he needs it but not in all circumstances. A hammer is a ***good*** tool, but for fixing a microchip it is an ***inappropriate*** tool. He must eventually expand his mind from a me-based survival mode and reach out to other people in we-based companionships. If he never finds a balance between personal desires and the needs of others around him, he will grow old still demanding his survival ***over*** others and pursuing a permanent state of desire, as so many people do in this world today.

I-go expands the following mind rafts:

A sense of 'self' in all things that divides 'me' from 'you' and 'this' from 'that'

A sense of possession: that things are 'mine' and not 'yours'

A sense of 'me-first': justifying the survival of 'me' over 'you' and 'this' over 'that'

It contracts the following:

A sense of unity: seeing yourself in everything and everything in yourself

A sense of faith: the feeling that things will be OK even if we don't manage, plan and control

A sense of collective responsibility: a connection to the needs of the tribe and a responsibility for helping to achieve them

As you will note, the three primary mind rafts that i-go expands are hardly the most community spirited, are they? That's because i-go is essentially a child's survival tool and the perceived advantages of values applied to achieve survival are very different from those of an adult, who has cooperative, community and family values to consider, not just survival. A baby's values are an essential survival mechanism motivating them to experience as much of the world as quickly as they can but they also need to learn to grow out of them or else the values of the world will remain no more mature than those of a baby.

Unfortunately, the modern world does not encourage you to grow out of immature mind rafts as quickly as it demands you grow up. Indeed, you are actually encouraged to retain the child's i-go and expand it as one of life's tools for success. This occurs because i-go ***seems*** to be a real thing, permanently a part of you and this is why it is so much relied upon as the foundation of everything we do. Yet I-go has no permanence. Like everything else in the natural world, it obeys the laws of transience. I-go is merely a facet of your personal truth, an unconscious context that filters your every thought, word and action. It ghosts in and out of your thinking, arising and falling dependant upon the situation. It is not really 'you' at all.

If you take a moment to listen to your i-go, the person you think you are, you will see what I mean. Were you to live your day in awareness of yourself, you would quickly realize that you are actually little more than a set of learned reactions. Like a boxer responding to the bell, you react in i-go mode to the world around you, employing the mind rafts burned into your personal truth and expanding them in your reality. If you want a different reality, you are going to have to listen to a different chime.

As you read this, for example, there is probably very little ego in you but if you suddenly come across a statement that challenges your core personal truth, a blast of i-go may erupt to defend what you believe to be '***my*** truth', '***my*** sense of values', '***my*** opinion'. You may become indignant, angry, insulted and, in your mind, the person who is challenging your reality will miraculously transform into an idiot, a liar, impertinent or mad. When something perceived to be 'me' or 'mine' is challenged, i-go expands within you to defend it. You get upset. You feel angry. Why does this happen? Because i-go is really just a conditioned self-defense mechanism to protect what you believe to be real and the mind rafts of division and independence are the seeds that ensure it flourishes within you in adulthood.

I regularly observe this reaction in my child's behavior, such as when he wants a toy someone else is playing with, when he cannot touch something he wants to touch, or when he is hungry and demands to be fed. His i-go is always on the prowl pushing the boundaries of what he can do and demanding his possessions, his rights or his current need be fulfilled. That is how he explores, learns and conditions his mind through the environment his mother and I create around him. But I also see this same reaction in every company I have consulted with, every person I coach and every client I work with, not least within myself. The judgment, emotion and linear thinking that nourishes i-go claims I am right, therefore you must be wrong. Thus i-go thrives beyond childhood in every boardroom, parliament building, factory floor and nightclub in the world. When the conditions of independence and separation exist in the mind, i-go drives the machine.

Since you were a child, permanence and division have been fused into your personal truth in the form of i-go like the tracks of your car are imprinted into a mud road. You have learned to protect what is yours, to seek permanent states of joy and differentiate between one thing and another rather than connecting them together. As you have grown into adulthood your mind begins to become less fluid, less impressionable and therefore less open to learn new things. You become even surer of who you are and even more in denial of the natural state of transience that denies the very existence of self. The old patterns start to stick because the influences needed to build group connectivity and contract i-go are not present in your environment. Just like the mud drying on the road, the tire tracks of your past conditioning remain impressed into your personal truth, causing you to react in ways that seem natural and appropriate but are actually just learned responses arising from your conditioned childhood consciousness. You have become trapped within your personal truth and to break free from this mental prison you must begin to see the universe for how it really is. If you did this, the conditions to expand i-go would not and could not exist.

It is like tending to flower seeds with water, nutrients and sunlight. If you do this, the flowers bloom automatically and in their own time. In the same way, a mind conditioned to see permanence and division in everything automatically grows i-go. It is fertile soil indeed. The great difference is that even a child can tell you how a flower grows but few intelligent adults have any inkling of what i-go is or how it expands. The average adult's notion of from where i-go is derived is no more mature than the child who believes they were borne to earth in the mouth of a stork. Yet were we to emerge from our spiritual slumber and open our minds to the true face of i-go, the connected awareness would be so powerful that it would portend freedom from suffering for all human beings

It should therefore be nothing less than frightening to you that i-go has become such a comfortable houseguest. You feel no sense of alarm or outrage against this squatter who has taken up residence inside the home of your mind. Indeed, such is his status that you have become the servant, rushing around after him trying to fulfill his every desire for uninterrupted pleasure, fulfillment of pride and avoidance of embarrassment. In order to adjust this intolerable situation you must first realize that i-go is only a predisposition. You have alternatives. You have actually worked very, very hard to nurture your i-go until you have become unfamiliar with the possibility of any other mental environment. Were you to spend but a fraction of the time you have invested in your i-go in the process of removing it from your mind, the entire world would change around you.

When novice monks are raised in temples in Tibet, for example, their i-go develops very differently from the average child brought up in the choke and smoke of a city with its contrasting influences. Sitting daily to explore the boundaries of human nature causes any child to condition very different seeds within their mind than the child raised on TV wrestling, video games and school yard jealousies. When different seeds are tended to, different fruits arise. If we want violent, aggressive, unsociable human beings, teach them to nourish the i-go with which they are born, teach them to fuel the divisions between you and me, teach them selfhood and to hoard their possessions and demonstrate as adults a perceived advantage in being self-***ish*** not self-***less***. But if we want peaceful compassionate, loving children....well, you know the rest.

Your brain comes hot-wired with i-go software from birth but the software should be upgraded and your brain reformatted as you mature. Sadly, few of us learn to leave the childhood i-go behind. We continue to be burdened by it. As the nomadic human discovered in ages past, when we are immersed in the interconnection and interdependence upon which nature thrives the world naturally inspires us to shed i-go but our urban cities shield people from this transformational experience and lock them into wholly different patterns. Ancient cultures had rites of passage designed to evolve i-go and immerse the mind in universal spirituality such as 'walkabout' in Australia or 'dream quest' in the native North American cultures. Our modern world is isolated from this reality because we have chosen to reject it in favor of the tangible and logical. Rather, we live in i-go-based environments, competitive neighborhoods, the dog-eat-dog business world and poverty-stricken communities created by an obsession with 'I', 'me' and 'mine'. While our environment demands we fight for dear life we quite readily mortgage boundless spiritual captial to invest in the stark physical quest for survival.

The I-Go-Based World

Never before was there a time in history when the products of i-go were so highly cherished. Sometimes subtly and sometimes not so subtly, i-go fuels all forms of global 'progress', fighting at the vanguard of even our most noble ambitions. It defines the future of humankind as much as it already haunts our past and all our creations of the present. Political leaders, silver screen stars, sports ambassadors, super models and high-flying business tycoons make great careers from their i-go but, like any addiction, i-go is ***dangerous***, especially when you are unaware that you are an addict. It has disseminated some of the most perilous misconceptions, bound countless millions of otherwise powerful people to an impotence built from self-ignorance and left planet earth teetering on the brink of an environmental catastrophe that threatens to send us all back to the Stone Age. And it did all this pretending to be our ***friend***. In this light, it serves us all to know a little more about the nature of i-go, what it creates in our world and why it endures so strongly.

The entrepreneur Donald Trump once suggested that the only people he had ever met without ego were losers. There's a perception for you. I wonder how many enlightened losers he has met? Expanding a sense of 'self', of personal possession and 'me-first' results in the current world. I-go loads our values with the perceived advantage of looking out for number one and valuing competition over cooperation. While Mr. Trump and the world's most economically blessed are convinced that i-go is a force for human advancement, this is a choice to select the illusion of physical strength over that of true spiritual power. In reality, i-go is no more a viable value system by which to seek personal contentment than it is a viable social system for unity. It is the philosophy of the child bully. Unless you are the bully, it is not much fun for anyone else.

The world's economic model serves as the finest ambassador for the merits of i-go but is also the greatest testimony to its flaws, hypocrisies and hollow promises. We have become besotted with competition as the finest fuel for economic prosperity but it is like choosing ice cream at every meal. While ice cream is nice, it becomes sickening if we eat it all the time. Like any idea, competition has its uses but it also has its limits. While competition may inspire individual greatness in such pursuits as sport, economic competition is not such a healthy application of the concept. It creates super-rich winners but hoards of impotent losers. The largest company or country simply gobbles up the others and eventually monopolizes markets and dictates choice. We see this in so many industries like automakers, oil, computer software, grocery stores, banks etc. Eventually, economic competition breaks down into monopolization, which is surely the antithesis of its purpose.

It is a violation of natural laws to claim that two companies in competition with one another have more power or resources to innovate and develop than two cooperating towards a mutually beneficial goal. Natural synergy guarantees that cooperation is more powerful than competition. Moreover, natural symbiosis says that win-win is a more effective choice than win-lose. But how many of us are seriously taught how to cooperate and work effectively as a team in society or at work? It is also false to claim that human beings are naturally more competitive than cooperative. It all depends on the mind rafts your environment has stimulated within you. Strong i-go's fear cooperation because they must drop their defenses and rely upon others. The resulting vulnerability is dangerous to an i-go that feels safest when it believes it is in control and independent of other people.

The child i-go demands physical safety first and foremost, so if we do not expand our consciousness beyond this limitation and begin to perceive the subtle advantage of teamwork in our search for personal survival, power and strength will always be perceived as primarily physical matters; being fit, resilient, self-sufficient and ensuring personal economic survival. Cooperative tendencies, while complimentary to this, are also conflicting. They require that we rely upon others, become inclusive, open our minds and awaken our spiritual capacity to empathize and be charitable, but the i-go often judges these traits as weaknesses. It rejects what cannot be seen, touched or measured, relying on the physical world to define reality. Unfortunately, like the oak tree in a storm, physical strength is not always an advantage. A palm tree bends but survives many environmental pressures whereas the oak tree may snap. There is much within our environment that suggests tempering our i-go's in the same way would result in a greater flexibility, community and inclusivity in all areas of life.

Within companies, sharing of ideas, work and resources between departments and people is universally recognized as essential for success. So why has it not become essential in society? What has become of the sense of tribal unity that values sharing over personal property and hoarding resources? We remain highly cautious of it. The author Marvin Weisbord said, *"Teamwork is the quintessential contradiction of a society grounded in individual achievement."* When I consult with companies regarding their teamwork, I am quick to make this point. We are not taught the values of cooperation and must adopt an entirely different value system to that we have learned outside business. They are alien to our nature because the command and control mindset of the industrial age has acquired a perceived advantage over cooperation and collaboration. While we teach our children to share their toys we seem to encourage adults to hoard as many personal possessions as we can in order to drive the global economy by means of the spiral of desire and aversion. The nice-to-have value system clashes with the practical-to-have values we actually live by.

What fuels this perceived advantage, dear reader? It is surely not faith. It is fear. Our lives are marinating in fear and we are drenched through with it. The great bogeyman awaits us all in the hidden demon of debt, public embarrassment, terrorism, Hell, loneliness, rejection; you name it. I-go shrouds the raft of fears that exist in our perpetually changing reality. So, in managing and controlling change we create the illusion that we are somehow the designer of our life, not the voyeur of circumstances mostly beyond our control. We purchase insurance to pay for the very chaos we know will befall us in this world. We invest in property in order to secure our futures with assets that have a false value imposed upon them. We seek financial independence in order to be the masters of our economic destiny, afraid that we cannot pay our debts, will not achieve the position that will pay for our dreams, petrified that we will lose our jobs, afraid that we will get too old and fall through the cracks in the system, afraid that we are not good enough, beautiful enough, wise enough, whatever it may be to maintain the illusion of control using the tool of fear.

When you participate in win-lose competition, when you seek to control, when you act in fear of the invisible threat, these are the trademarks of i-go. You hand over your personal power to an illusion. The mind rafts that create it are the results of someone else's misguided perception of reality and, I can tell you with some certainty, that they were not contented or peaceful minds. They were afraid, felt powerless and desired the enduring status quo so they did not have to believe in world of perpetual change. If your ambition is self-discovery, contentment and liberation from suffering, these are not the mind rafts I would recommend you choose for your journey.

I-go is not strength. It is the absolute illusion of strength. It is force, not power. My i-go can force you to respect me through control and abuse but I can never attain the infinitely more valuable power of your respect, cooperation and commitment through force. With respect you will do anything for me, not because I am in control, but because I would do anything for you. I-go contracts authentic power through the illusion of force, it contracts authentic faith through the illusion of control, it contracts authentic courage through the illusion of fear. In contrast, responsibility, courage and faith are the three most powerful attitudes in which you can ever invest for they emanate from a source that is spirit-based, not i-go based.

Focus Model

I-Go-Based Passion	Spirit-Based Passion
Fear-Based	Trust-Based
High Threat/Low Challenge	Low Threat/High Challenge
Creates Conformity	Creates Alignment of Purpose
Extracts Mediocrity	Extracts Excellence
Disempowers Individuals	Empowers Individuals
Causes Fragmentation	Promotes Harmony
Generates Stagnancy	Generates Change
Creates Paradigm Prisoners	Creates Paradigm Pioneers
Shames and Blames	Recognizes and Celebrates
Exclusive	Inclusive
Encourages Myopic Thinking	Encourages Creative & Innovative Thinking
Externally Motivates	Internally Motivates
Traditional	Transformational

This Focus Model has been adapted from Bill Gould's Transformational Thinking and perfectly illustrates the contrasting results you will achieve when focusing your purpose on i-go objectives or spirit-based objectives. The passion of i-go is forceful indeed but it is a negative motivation, powered by fear and threat. It disempowers you and locks you into a paradigm from which fear disables liberation. It expands thinking that is shortsighted and limiting. In comparison, spirit-based passion is the motivation of human achievement, not avoidance. It begins with trust and seeks to inspire excellence in people, promoting the exponential power produced through harmonious synergies of effort aligned in purpose and intention.

The ubiquity of competitive mind rafts in global systems such as economics, democracy, law and education have convinced people that they must be in some way profound but what alternatives have we mustered? In everything but name, you are conditioned to a world that insists you will fail without i-go driving your success. You have learned that, without placing your own safety and comfort above others, it is likely that you will be less safe and less comfortable than others. You believe that without the authority and power to control people around you and the events that transpire in your life, you will be at the mercy of other people and a neurotic natural reality that punishes the uneducated and the weak. This is not the only reality available to you. When you choose to sit and listen to the options revealed by a still mind, you will know that. We must all make a new choice to clean the home not house the i-go squatter who has taken residence there.

Does the perpetual struggle to ensure your own survival economically, relationally, through your status, position and general feeling of self-worth really serve the purpose of your contentment? Of course it doesn't but you have probably given up struggling against it. It seems normal, inevitable, ***easy***. The vast majority of the Western world's populace has accepted these issues as '***the system***', too vast to be affected by an individual's insignificant contribution to life. But this is a cop-out. Throw out the squatter, tear down the walls of your i-go and suddenly you find the true source of your fear lying buried in your subconsciousness: "What lies beyond those walls?" This can be more scary than it seems. Like the prisoner whose cell door is thrown open after a life of incarceration, the fear of an unknown freedom may be greater than the suffering common for a comfortable captive.

While the global populace attempts to accommodate i-go by designing it into our life's ambitions and fears, we continue to expand desire and aversion not liberation from the roots of our suffering. That is how most of us have attempted to solve our problems. We are motivated by i-go and not by spirit and are running scared, not from a real threat but from a perceived one that just keeps growing. Your mind *is* your reality and it is a reality that has become so full with the possessions of a squatter that you can no longer see the walls, the ceiling, the floor, the controlling limits that have been built within an infinite space. I-go is a choice to remain ignorant of your mature self and to reside within the mind of the child you were born into. I-go is not you. It is not yours. It shadows in and out of your reality, strengthened every time you perceive a separation, disconnect from someone or seek personal success at the expense of others around you. You are free to choose awareness or non-awareness, mindfulness or mindlessness, the child mind or the mature mind. You can remain separate and accept a reality of eroding trust, deepening disrespect and expansion of suffering that is the inevitable result of valuing i-go, or you can choose awareness and clean the home that needs no guest. For the home is who you are, not the guest within it. Ego is a fruit of the mind not the mind itself but it need no more be a fruit of the mind than a fist need be a product of the hand.

Chapter 6

Uni-time and Emotional Rebirth

"We are healed from suffering only by experiencing it to the full."
Marcel Proust – French Novelist, Essayist and Critic
(1871 - 1922)

Uni-time

Your greatest power in this world is to create change here and now. This is 'real time' creation, and mastery of this skill is the surest means of liberating yourself from suffering. Unfortunately, most people do not live in the present and deprive themselves of the chance. Living at other times, mulling future aspirations or cursing past events that have captured residual pain dissipates much of your creative energy. Dreams are great targets and memories are fabulous to integrate into better mind rafts but they can become powerful burdens too. You begin seeking peace at some other time than now, desiring a larger pay packet, finding the right partner, achieving a professional goal or avoiding a painful or undesirable situation. While you live life in the spiral of suffering, placing conditions on when and where peace and contentment will be attained, you become distracted from your happiness because you make it conditional on some future objective. Wouldn't it be better to adjust your perception of time so that you understand, quite categorically, that peace must exist ***now*** or it will never exist at all? A life lived in such a way is a life lived in provolution.

Does your current mind raft of tri-part time (past, present and future) serve your life purpose or expand your suffering? Take your perception of past events as an example. If you believe that the past is dead and gone, all those painful memories you have of people and events will appear like fixed recordings that can never be re-edited or transformed. Every time you recall them they trigger your suffering. Trauma, heartbreak and anxiety replay endlessly as a lodestone carried into your future. This reaction is the result of perceiving time as separate from you, not a part of you. It is up to you to change that and start using your past, not as a dead weight, but as a living education of who you are and what you will inevitably become if you continue to attract the same things into your life. In this chapter you will learn how ***uni-time*** connects your past and future together ***now***, where all creation occurs. By living in uni-time you can recondition any past trauma and continue unburdened into a better future.

The very idea of tri-part time is more than a little silly when you think about it. Take a piece of string representing your current day: how would you divide it up so that one part represents the past, one represents the present and the last one represents the future? It would be easy to divide the past and future pieces but how long would the present piece be? How long is 'now'? The problem with measuring 'now' is that it is over before it begins. It has no shape or size. Despite this, both your past and your future begin now so it is vital to become intimately acquainted with the present if you want to be pro-active about either. Doesn't tri-part time remind you of how i-go divides and separates one thing from the next?

Secondly, tri-part time is measured ***outside*** of you. It is based upon the rotation of the earth and its passage around the sun, which seems a very fixed, cyclic and dependable mechanism. But remember what Poincaré discovered about seemingly predictable systems? In a few billion years the earth may very well not be here, so would time end because there is nothing to rotate or travel around the sun? Of course not. Time never really began. Your watch is measuring the speed of rotation of the planet in 24 parts called 'one day'. Imagine if we used other natural processes as measuring gauges for time like the life of bumble bee or the duration of a tropical storm. They are no more a gauge of time than the earth's rotation. The perception of time that is commonly held is not a real thing, any more than i-go is a real thing. The external projection of time ignores how we really ***experience*** it. Inside you, me and everyone else, time occurs at very different speeds according to what we are doing and how we feel. If bored, an hour lasts an eternity, right? When engrossed in something interesting, time flies by in an instant. Thus, time can be seen as an internal perception, not fixed or objective.

Lastly, based upon the traditional tri-part model of time, we perceive events as happening in a linear progression: A to B to C etc. This is like a set of dominoes falling into one another. The first domino hits the second, the second hits the third and so on. We can relate to the cause and the effect because we see the linear sequence of hitting and falling. We can also connect how the first domino falling over is a cause of the last one falling over but logic suggests that the last domino can not have been the cause of the first falling over or any of the events that happened before the last one fell. Universal interconnectivity and interdependence disputes this impression of time moving forward, as we have learned in a previous chapter; but to understand why uni-time connects everything to the present moment, you need to understand how your body, mind and energy systems interdependently bring your entire history right here, right now.

Science says everything in the universe comes from energy that can neither be created nor destroyed. From the pages of this book to the dolphins in the sea, from the planets of our solar system to the sun that bathes us in its light, the energy that is all things is also the ***potential*** transforming one thing into another. You are made of energy too and life has provided you with a personal bank vault of potential from which to create your life in whatever energetic form you wish to experience it. The energy of people, places, objects, thoughts, words and actions converge in your present like threads woven together to form an energetic ***'presence'*** that influences and affects the future you are creating now.

You may wonder at the storage space on your home computer's hard drive but ***you*** are a far superior and infinitely more accurate recording device. The thermal, chemical, electrical and kinetic energy pulsing through your body is a chronicle of your entire personal history. Everything you have ever thought, said, felt, done or experienced is recorded in your physical cells, in your mind, in your hormonal secretions and in the energetic body that surrounds and flows through you. You are a transmitter of all you have done, drawing towards you everything that responds to the beacon of who you are.

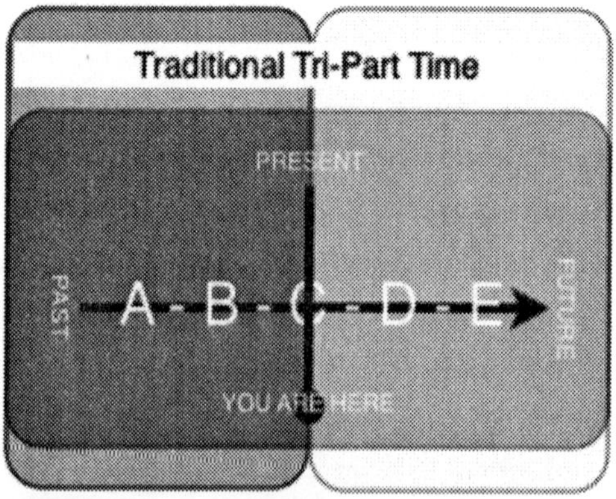

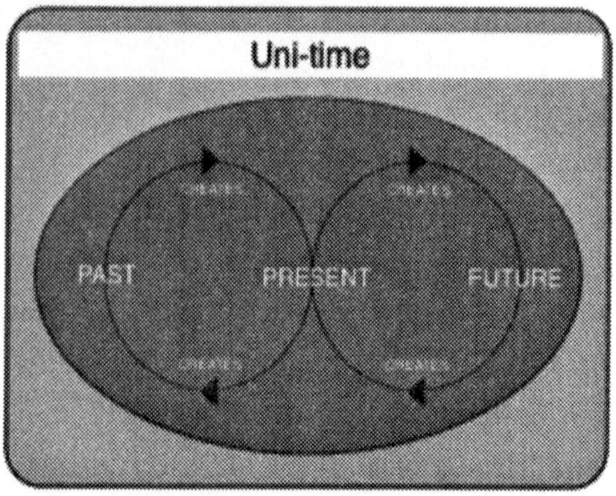

This means that the past never passes. It never dies. It never fades away. It pulses within you at all times. When you wonder how that final domino can influence the first, your energetic body explains this mechanism. An event when I was aged five has changed now that I am 21 (cough, cough) and is still changing today because I project my memory of past events according to my current perception, not the perception that I held when I was five years old. Your memories are not prerecorded movies, they are actually re-edited every time you repeat them, adding different music, different plots, even changing the actors. In the same way that two different people will have different opinions of the same foods, so, at two different times in your life you project two very different perceptions of the same event, as if you were two different people also. This is not the result of an inaccurate recording mechanism (the mind), as psychologists or biologists might explain, it is a result of the most accurate reflection of who you are at any given moment: your perception.

"But hold on," you scream, "I was angry at my father when I was 18 and I am still angry at him today! Not all feelings and events change!" Let's understand why that is. Rather than time being a linear process outside of you, uni-time is like a cocktail poured into your energetic body, comprised from the energy of your entire life history. Individual life events add their different energetic flavors to the cocktail giving it a unique overall taste responsible for the general trends you experience in your life. As life passes and you add anger, jealousy, joy, love or any other emotional energy to your present experience it affects the taste of the entire cocktail. People tend to become more and more fixed in their ways as they grow older and begin repeating traits and reactions that bias the emotional cocktail in their most familiar flavors. Like the tire tracks hardening into the mud as it dries on the road, perception grows ever more biased towards these 'standardized' reactions. Thus as you look back through your personal history, some events will begin to ***appear*** fixed, as tri-part time claims they should be, but they are not. What is actually happening is that you are fixing your mind so that your memory is no longer being allowed to naturally adapt. Your i-go has claimed your emotions as 'mine' and the event as 'me', thus, the event seems to be over, leaving you a victim of your past.

If you perceive your personal history as fixed and finished in tri-part time, this is incredibly disempowering. You inhibit your ability to liberate yourself from the roots of your suffering, believing the roots beyond your reach, past and finished. They are not. The empowering choice is to understand that your entire history still exists inside you, around you, within your every cell and sinew. You can learn how to adapt your present attitude to heal the past and create the freedom that you seek. Living in uni-time, you take back the power to change the energetic presence you are creating and, by doing so, transform past, present and future simultaneously.

Emotional Rebirth

The entire point of life is sensual experience. Whatever you think, see, feel, touch, taste, hear or intuit is translated by your perception into physical emotion. You then have a choice to make: you can believe your emotions are 'you' and thus react to them as 'me' and 'mine', or you can learn how to observe what you are attracting into your life and let go of the resulting mental, emotional, physical and spiritual suffering.

Let me be very clear when I say that your emotional reactions to events are not random sensual fits. They are neither abstract nor is your response to them 'ordinary'. Your emotions are personal and unique reactions to your present state of conditioning stimulated by your environment. You have ***learned*** to be angry, to be frustrated, to be jealous, to be afraid, because your i-go believes there is a 'me' to be frustrated, to be jealous, to fear. Your emotional reactions represent the purest undiluted impression of who you really are and why you suffer in your own unique way. If you continue to grasp at these emotions as the child, in i-go and the belief that they are 'me' and 'mine', you will continue to grasp at an illusion that conditions suffering to recur. But, if you can learn to observe and let emotions come and go without attachment, you can recondition them to become their true purpose: signposts on your process of spiritual growth.

In my therapies, so many people attribute their suffering to 'normal family problems', 'ordinary cultural conditioning', 'feelings common for people my age' or other stereotypes that they have accepted as personal truth. They possess their emotional suffering like a skin donned as a social obligation, a victim of their society. Other people adopt emotions as dark trophies in the cabinet of their personal history, points in time to which they can relate and which rationalize their current self-perception. These memories become the justification for abiding self-hurt, justifying pain or even subconsciously serving the purpose of self-sabotage in some way, rationalizing unhappiness and an enduring lack of success.

Traumatic past events are like forces of gravity in your life, great weights anchoring your present mind to them and influencing the intentions, words and actions by which you react in the here and now. The power of these events pins your present moment to past times, like a piece of historical cloth being drawn along the ground and snagging on rough experiences. The more rough experiences you cling to as 'mine' the more snags you accumulate. You have not learned to let go nor have you learned the value of doing so. Every painful event therefore becomes an energetic boulder that has happened to 'me', that is 'mine' and the emotional baggage takes on a greater and greater role of defining who you are. Thus, in uni-time, you exist in the present moment bathed in an emotional cocktail of past trauma. The question is: 'How do you exist unburdened in the here and now?'

Begin by looking at your emotional reaction to an event as a reflection of who you are, not a reflection of the event itself. Two people will feel differently when they experience the same event, so, if you should begin perceiving your personal reaction as a reflection of yourself, you can stop blaming the event and start doing something about the feeling. It is like when you stub your toe against a chair and kick the chair in frustration. It wasn't really the chair's fault, was it? If you believe emotions are caused by events, then you will always kick the chair and render yourself impotent to change how you feel. Being a victim of your own emotional states is not a great way to seek a peaceful life.

The key to taking responsibility for your emotions begins by understanding what happens inside you when emotion erupts. When you experience a traumatic event, where does the emotion come from and why do different people react differently to the same event? People say things like "He really makes me angry", or "I hate bigots," but these reactions are neither 'normal' nor 'human', they are simply yours. ***You*** have created them. Other people will not get angry with the same person or be biased towards or against the same character traits. Changing how you feel about the world around you begins by changing your responsibility for your feelings.

In his book 'Anger', the Vietnamese Buddhist Monk Thich Nhat Hanh pens a great analogy describing how most people handle strong emotions when they arise. He talks about a fire being set by an arsonist and the victim chasing the arsonist rather than putting out the fire. It is a wonderful metaphor for how we prefer to blame someone else for our feelings and hunt them down in order to get into an emotional (or even physical) tussle rather than accepting that all emotions arise from within us and the suffering they cause is ours alone to address. If a fire is burning within you, who supplies the fuel in the first place? As Thich Nhat Hanh so rightly suggests, putting out the fire within you is a far wiser course of action than running after the perpetrator while your house burns to the ground. Indeed, as much as possible removing the fuel for the fire is even wiser.

If you begin to treat emotions as living energy, you will begin to perceive their fuel for what it really is: i-go. Emotions are born, grow, mature and die in a life cycle, just like expanding and contracting mind rafts. Unfortunately, many of us have a hard time letting them contract and die away, reacting to a strong emotional stimulus with a mental firestorm that dispenses shame and blame for the event. 'He did it', 'She didn't do that', 'I could've done this', the 'coulda-woulda-shoulda' game gets under way. You may endlessly play this game in your mind, cursing or praising the protagonists, reliving what you wished you'd said or engrossing yourself in how the outcome was just or tragic. Emotional energy then ***expands*** through your own little mind game, rather than contracting by letting emotional energy mature and fade away through observation of it. Can you see how the 'clinging' reaction to an emotion as 'mine' removes you from the moment of uni-time and places you in a mental state where you are no longer the observer, but the owner or the '***becomer***' of the emotion? Even though it doesn't start out as 'me or 'mine' you quite literally become one with it as you allow the head to 'manage' your reaction and attach to emotions as being a part of who you think you are through the i-go's intellectualization of unintelligible events.

The external event that triggers an emotional response is irrelevant. It could be anything. The potential for it lies dormant within your own energetic body like an egg, awaiting an event outside that will trigger the 'hatching' reaction inside you so that you can experience it. If a particular past event made you very angry and you have rationalized your anger as justified, you will have held onto that anger and added it to your energetic body. You 'become' Mr. Angry. Every time you recall that memory, you will thus recreate the same sensation of anger because that is what you have now squirreled away as your personal possession.

Now that it is a part of your energetic fingerprint, your energy body will naturally attract future opportunities to release the anger energy because it does not belong to you. As more opportunities to feel angry arise you may keep choosing to stoke the anger in your energetic body, empowering the spiral of suffering with more power to repeat over and over again but, as we shall learn in the next chapter, this can cause great physical pain and even death. To transcend your conditioning you must be prepared to ***recondition*** your energetic body to release your emotional belongings, a process that can only happen with sensitivity to who you are and how you are feeling right here and now.

The question you must come to terms with is not whether your emotional reaction is warranted or deserved; it is whether you ***choose*** to feel angry or not. Is your reality better served by clinging to the justifications for the anguish, fear, hatred, despair or frustration that has been integrated into your energetic body or is your only choice of escape to recondition what has been stamped into you like a seal into hot wax?

I vividly remember returning from India when I was around 20 years of age, after attending a Buddhist retreat in Dharamsala. Having found the ultimate truth at such a young age (that's irony by the way), and fresh with the zeal of a convert I felt compelled to discuss the concept of conditioning with one of my older brothers, suggesting that reconditioning the mind would remove the roots of all suffering, even his. I recall that my brother was more than a little skeptical of the notion that I might consider 'brainwashing' as the solution to my woes. I remarked that we were all 'brainwashed', to use his term, and it is only the choice between which brainwashing we choose. Yet, he was unconvinced by this argument. He felt that, somehow, intelligent minds naturally find truth and that any concerted attempt to adjust the course of it or recondition it for a different purpose was somehow a perversion or a manipulation. Today, with global conditioning so much more sophisticated than it was 20 years ago it is even clearer to me that we are all conditioned with mind rafts that predispose us to certain reactions, particularly emotionally, and to do something about them is to first accept that who we are today can only be adjusted through a concerted effort to change who we are today. It is the nature of mind that truth is personal, not absolute and to create a mind at peace we must be prepared to let go of the conditioning that realizes in us all such a strong sense of 'me' and open up enough space for selflessness to grow.

Powerful emotional experience offers you the opportunity to adapt your reaction in the present and thus create a different you on which to build a new future, or to reinforce the same reactive patterns that guarantee the continuous reproduction of your past. That is the enormous power of free will. The emotional pain and bliss of life is the carrot and the stick gently prodding you towards greater self-discovery. Sensitivity to your emotional state in the present moment utilizes emotional energy as a boundless opportunity for self-exploration, not for suffering. There are numerous practices and habits that can help you achieve this, which I do not have space to go into in any great detail in this book. However, one wonderful practice is Emotional Freedom Technique (EFT). It has been receiving high kudos for its quick, painless method of opening up emotional blockages by a simple tapping technique, which can be learned in just a few minutes. It reveals how our emotional responses can be relieved simply by tapping key energy points in the body to achieve long and lasting freedom from phobias, conditioned reactions and even physical pain. I strongly advise visiting the website *www.emofree.com* where you will find a free download to teach yourself this amazing technique.

Yet there is also no substitute for sustained self-awareness, best achieved through meditative techniques that help soothe the mind and body in numerous ways. Awareness and sensitivity to one's own state of mind is an essential ingredient for the relief of suffering for it attunes us to the present moment and allows emotions to arise and fall naturally, unhindered, as they should. During the course of a day you will have hundreds of opportunities to catch yourself reacting and to train your awareness on your feelings instead. Although this may initially seem somewhat alien to you if you have never practiced any awareness techniques, daily practices such as meditation, qigong or certain martial arts are purposefully centered around self-awareness, breathing and sensitivity, each a means of living in the present moment. Expanding your spiritual routine by adopting your practice within your daily routine slowly calms your mind until it is able to settle and attain stillness in the present moment. In this state, your feelings will become more vibrant. As emotions arise, your attention will turn to them as an observer, not a participant. You will be aware of them expanding inside you but refuse participation in them. As you experience an emotion from the position of detachment you will feel it expand to a maximum point and then naturally contract. You need not become the net to catch them as they are passing through you. All things pass, and as you learn to detach from emotions regularly, their period of expansion will decrease, their contraction will accelerate and your mind will return to a more placid state more frequently and for longer periods.

Awareness is ultimately the only choice you make. Are you willing to be aware of who you are, how you feel, what you have created and what you can potentially create? If you are, then this is a commitment to be yourself unflinchingly, unapologetically, in love with the moment and courageous enough to live life in unitime.

Chapter 7

Physical Health

"It is no measure of health to be well adjusted to a profoundly sick society."

Jiddu Krishnamurti - Indian Writer, Speaker and Spiritual Philosopher (1895 – 1986)

Putting Something In to Take Something Out

Allopathic medicine, the predominant Western approach to physical health, is consistent with the Western perception of the universe as a whole. The human body is viewed like a machine made of parts and pieces, each distinct and separate from the next. In contrast, the word 'wellness' is often used to describe Eastern health methodologies and it signifies an important distinction between the ideological premise separating the two. Whereas health is usually considered a physical and/or mental state, wellbeing is our complete physical, mental, emotional, energetic and spiritual states combined. Although we can be physically fit, if we are stuck in a cycle of suffering that continuously produces emotional stress we cannot be said to be truly *well*.

In the final section of Part I, we are going to continue with our theme on energy and discuss the human body as an energy system. We will examine how the energy of our personal truth transforms and integrates into our physical body. Whereas we can easily create the appearance of good physical health through drugs and surgery, wellbeing requires sensitivity to the indivisible nature of mind and body. The interconnectivity of these two energy systems should encourage us to seek health and wellbeing through daily practice of modalities specifically designed to nurture and refine energy.

Western medicine uses an allopathic system to heal people. According to The American Heritage Dictionary, 'allopathy' is the means of *"treating physical disease with remedies that produce effects different from those that caused the disease itself"*. While this may sound fairly obvious, it is also rather a strange way to solve any problem. If your computer keeps getting viruses what is the best way to ensure that you stop getting them? You might answer that you should install anti-virus software but this is precisely the way in which allopathic medicine acts to remove disease. It adds a solution that slows your machine down, gets in the way and adds a certain degree of inconvenience to your computing life. The best way to stop viruses is to catch the virus maker, the real cause of your problem.

The allopathic approach to sickness is not unlike many other approaches we take to problems in life. We do not seek root causes because they are subtle or we refuse to look beyond the boundaries of our own perception for the places they may hide. An example of this is the Western justice system in which we jail the perpetrators of crime, removing the effect, but do not address the roots of social disquiet that conditioned the individual. Clearly it is more complex a solution to rethink an entire social model than it is to blame individuals for their actions but we have already learned how one conditions the other. While we should not remove responsibility for actions from the individual, we would do well to query the degree to which an individual's environment predisposes him or her to certain character traits that are virtually inevitable. Sometimes all that it takes to find a better solution is an expansion of our awareness to reveal deeper root causes that imply alternative solutions.

Allopathic medicine creates a new effect to remove a current effect. If you imagine that every disease or sickness in your body has at least one cause, the approach of allopathic medicine is to introduce a secondary effect that produces the appearance of removing the cause. This may be a drug, which masks the cause or controls it, or surgery, which removes the part where the effect is most acute. What's the difference, you might ask? Allopathy creates the illusion of health, while true wellness is the creation of a life absent of any causes of dis-***ease***. Why doesn't allopathic medicine remove causes? Because firstly, in the vast majority of cases, Western medicine often does not know exactly why we get sick and secondly, the vested interest in maintaining the status quo is just too big a gravy train to slow down.

It is without doubt that allopathic medicine has a proven track record of results. As an ex-asthmatic, I have been kept alive by inhalers, so for that I am very grateful for its success. However, the USD $104 billion in drug research and development invested each year[3] provides an extremely lucrative motivation to maintain the allopathic approach and to ignore alternatives. In 2007, U.S. and Australian researchers reported that 25 per cent of doctors received some direct payment from drug companies and 94 per cent have *"at least one type of relationship with the drug industry"*,[4] which is a euphemism for receiving gifts of some sort. With such a profitable and incestuous relationship between the suppliers of drugs and the doctors who prescribe them, it is inevitable that the appetite for alternatives is diminished.

We are led to believe that allopathic medicine is far more reliable than homeopathic or other alternatives, but exactly how safe and reliable is it? Medical institutions routinely attack and ridicule alternative and complimentary therapies as being quackery but there is a dark and dangerous side to allopathic medicine that is conveniently brushed under the carpet. Medical mistakes are rated by the Nutrition Institute of America as the highest contributor to death in the USA with 784,000 people dying annually compared to nearly 700,000 for heart disease and over 550,000 for cancer.[5] Despite these alarming statistics, the hundreds of billions of dollars spent on drugs and surgery each year and the saturation of lucrative Western-styled hospitals and clinics around the world is testimony to the public's faith in allopathic mind rafts.

The world has embraced quick fix Western economics, quick-fix pleasure, quick-fix surgery, quick-fix joy, so is it any wonder that we have embraced the same quick-fix approach to wellbeing through physical health? Our adrenalin-fueled lifestyles demand wellbeing at the speed of fast food and instant coffee. However, as we have seen in the spiral of suffering all solutions begin with sensitivity to a problem and awareness of its cause and so we must first be sensitive to the energetic properties we are expanding in our reality before we can be sure of which wellness solutions to expand and which to contract. ***Sustainable*** physical health will not be attained by introducing new effects into the body but by identifying the current energetic causes of your suffering and contracting their presence from your life. The problem for Western medicine is that it does not discern the physical body to have any energy system at all.

What if we opened our mind to the possibility that physical health is a reflection of the mental, emotional and environmental energy that we have given presence to in our reality? This would imply that our mental and emotional energies condition our body in the same way that it is conditioned by the energy of food or liquids. Physical sickness may be the manifestation of a virus or an infection but why do some people manifest symptoms and others don't? As we learned in the first chapter, scientific study has clearly demonstrated the connection between a strong immune system and a strong perception of one's future and current opportunities. Medical thinking is beginning to accept the mind, less as being a thought machine, and more a profound stimulus triggering physical effects in the flavor of our feelings. From this perspective, we can now consider the physical appearance of sickness in the human body as an energetic reflection of our state of mind and spirit. By excluding the possibility that poor health is the result of bad luck or the body 'going wrong' , we can explore the possibility that personal choice and the ability to self-regulate behaviors are primary factors determining good health. Rather than relying on doctors to fix us and drugs to fight off infection, this mind raft empowers us all to take responsibility for our personal health as part of a peaceful lifestyle. The journey to sustainable wellbeing is nothing less than a lifestyle choice.

A Way of Health or a Way of Life?

In the East, health has always been an issue of relationships. It is believed that neither the mind, nor the body, nor the spirit can be considered the sole cause or victim of sickness because each is an interconnected and interdependent part of the other. It is no coincidence that that the symbol of Tao came from China and that the yin-yang represents this paradoxical concept of opposites constituting all matter. Human health is not excluded from this paradox. In Eastern philosophy, wellbeing could never be divided into separate ideological niches as it is in the West. This would compromise a deeper understanding of 'what' is actually sick and 'why'. A holistic approach to health requires our acceptance of the principle that a healthy body cannot exist without a healthy energy system, spirit or mind and vice versa.

An Eastern medical practitioner will ponder a patient's medical condition from the perspective of how to help transform their personal traits and habits so that sick energetic patterns are not repeated. He will know that the very presence of these patterns has a profound physical impact and, in order to transform the person who exists in sickness into a person who exists in wellness, behaviors and beliefs must adapt through sustained practice of new habits. An Eastern doctor accepts that drugs alone cannot possibly remove the roots of sickness. How can you 'cure' something that has become a integral part of the patient? It is like trying to cure them of their eye or leg!

Secondly, as we will see when we take a closer look at traditional Chinese medicine (TCM) and chakra theory, from an Eastern perspective the onus of responsibility for wellness is placed squarely on the shoulder of the patient. Western doctors try to cure you when you are sick, but an Eastern doctor understands that the cure may simply mask the underlying cause of the problem and that lifestyle adjustments need to be made by the patient in order that sickness does not recur. It is simply negligent of any medical practitioner who is truly concerned for a person's wellbeing to dispense a solution without the patient having to do anything more than swallow. This is why Eastern methodologies contain meditative exercises, movement and a process of awareness expansion designed to help a person understand what and who is really sick and empower them to realize their own patterns of wellness. In his book 'Freedom' the tantric master Osho wonderfully contextualizes the absurdity of the Western health system. He wonders why we pay our doctor when we are sick. Wouldn't it make more sense to pay our health practitioners to keep us well? That would be the incentive for a change in perception that is needed to change our approach to wellness.

Although such practices as yoga, chi gong or meditation have become quite popular as wellness regimes across the world, the Western mind is thoroughly unaccustomed to the ritualistic philosophies from which they have been borrowed. Pharmaceuticals and surgery seem tangible to us but we are nonplussed by the notion that stretching or breathing with awareness can manifest greater long-term wellbeing than zapping viruses or chopping out malfunctioning body parts. Having said that, any health routine that espouses daily exercise, personal awareness and balanced diet sounds pretty attractive, even from a Western paradigm, which is exactly what many Eastern practices prescribe, but their assertion of an energy system within the body that is undetected by allopathic medicine is too far-fetched for the average Westerner to consider. If we accepted the existence of such a system, what would become of personal truth dedicated to the notion of proof over faith? Just as 'atomos' was the official reality of Greece, so the modern world adopts the 'see it before believing it' mentality towards health for it fits nicely with the physical laws in which we have invested so much of our personal truth. It is ironic that for 2000 years before Mendeleev the concept of atoms rested upon nothing more concrete than faith. Sadly, the regimens of the East are today tarred with an air of cultish irrationality by minds raised on a diet of physical proof and double-blind experiments. Yet, as quantum physics has proven, we might do well to open ourselves to the inevitability that the universe is full of illogical, intangible things which technology cannot yet decipher or detect. As Einstein said, *"Not everything that can be counted counts and not everything that counts can be counted."*

Evidence for the Human Energy Field (HEF)

Many people may view the human energetic body, as discussed in previous chapters, as being 'new age' but the ideas have been with us for thousands of years, if not tens of thousands. Once upon a time, science and traditional medicine shared a parallel perspective on life. Despite the prejudice that has grown in modern times, we are now entering a period where traditional healing therapies like acupuncture, energy healing, massage, Tai Chi and other such modalities are in the process of reconverging and reunifying with traditional science due to the mounting evidence that suggests the human energy field (HEF) is not some crackpot myth, but a real, quantifiable phenomenon that has a powerful influence on human health.

It is not a modern revelation that human cells generate electrical fields that can be detected on the skin's surface. The ECG heart monitor in a hospital is specifically designed to measure the electrical patterns emanating from the heart and the research for this instrument was reported to have begun in London's St. Bartholomew's hospital in 1872. The evidence for electrical activity in the brain, the forerunner of the EEG, is no less immature. A Liverpool physician called Richard Caton studied the cerebral hemispheres of rabbits and monkeys and published his findings in an 1875 edition of the British Medical Journal. So, it has long been suspected that measuring the body's electrical behavior is a means of diagnosing health. What is disputed is that the tiny magnetic fields generated by individual cells could cumulatively have any physiological significance to a person's overall state of health. While chaos may already have convinced the reader that small causes have very influential effects, unfortunately, this has often been ignored and ridiculed by those whose status relies upon the survival of the current paradigm. The tendency for human beings when encountering ideas that challenge perceived wisdom is to marginalize and denigrate them, which has occurred almost systemically with regard to HEF.

From Brahmanism to the Kabbalah, traditional Chinese medicine to Buddhism and Christianity, the presence of HEF has been hinted at either directly by its definition as chakras or meridians, which we will look at in greater detail shortly, or represented by depictions such as a halo painted around the heads of saints or prophets in religious interpretations. But evidence for HEF is not just anecdotal. As we shall see there is plenty of empirical data to engage our curiosity as to how our energetic system operates and to what extent it impacts upon our physical health. Nevertheless, we should not ignore the anecdotal just because it hails from sources in our ancient past. Accounts of HEF stretch back 5,000 years into recorded history, and, we can assume, far further into the mists of history than this considering the veneration with which the philosophies describing it are still held to this day. The technological success of science has buoyed an intellectual arrogance that our less technological ancient ancestors were naïve or gullible fools. We are assured that the passage of time and discoveries of science come together to create 'progress' and 'advancement', when the opposite may be true in matters essential to the pursuit of freedom and contentment. If our spiritual growth is the key to our contentment and we have discarded it as bogus and delusory, how advanced can we really claim to be? While science has led to an explosion in material desires, ancient wisdom sought the means by which to leave them behind and it did so by devising philosophies that described the great significance of the HEF in our wellbeing and by crafting practices that nurtured its development to attain liberation from suffering.

But what of modern science? Is HEF the invisible, undetectable imagination of minds longing for something supernatural, or an elegant natural framework into which snugly fits the entire ordinance for human wellbeing? Let's take a brief look at some of the more significant studies into HEF in order to illustrate to the reader that the HEF is not such weird science after all.

Although studies go back further, one of the most notable came in the mid-1800's when Count Von Reichenbach introduced the Odic field, an electrical aura he had detected around the human body that behaved with very similar characteristics to Maxwell's electromagnetic field. He described the field to be like a gas or a liquid but what was intriguing was that his description indirectly hinted at what Bohr and Heisenberg would demonstrate in the Copenhagen Interpretation many decades later. He suggested that the Odic field had both wave-like and particle-like properties. Count Von Reichenbach also claimed to have demonstrated, in accordance with yin-yang philosophy, that the positive and negative electrical charge corresponded with the right and left sides of the human body.

In his 1911 book *'The Human Atmosphere, or the Aura Made Visible by the aid of Chemical Screens'*, Walter Kilmer, a doctor from St. Thomas' Hospital in London, proposed that the human energy system was an indicator of health and mood. Through the use of 'Kilmer' screens, he trained people to see the auras surrounding people. When he dispensed with the screens, people had become attuned to auras and could still see them unaided.

The first photographic evidence of HEF didn't arrive until the 1940's when Russian scientist Dr. Semyon Kirlian and his wife Valentina began developing a technique now known as Kirlian photography. This technique didn't use a camera, but photographic film and a high-frequency oscillator. After starting on still photography of energy flashes around leaves and fingers, they developed an optical filter that allowed real-time observation of the phenomenon and observation of light shows erupting around their hands. By 1949, Kirlian photography claimed to detect diseases in plants that were undetectable by other means than their electrical discharges. Like Count Von Reichenbach, they also showed how the HEF images they were able to detect could provide people with an accurate depiction of their state of health, even of disease that was yet to reveal itself.

Depictions of heroes, prophets, religious leaders and rulers with halos around their heads can be traced back 3000 years to images of Ra in Egypt. The halo is a representation of a strong HEF emanating from the body and is connected with purity, strength and holiness. It is no coincidence that it is depicted around the head as this is usually the part of the body where energetically sensitive people will be able to view it most easily. Regardless, scientific evidence for HEF was scarce while the equipment to measure such subtle energy levels remained beyond the capabilities of science. In 1978, however, Dr. Richard Dobrin, Dr. John Pierrakos, and Barbara Brennan published their *'Instrumental Measurements of the Human Energy Field'*, in which they describe an experiment to measure the light fluctuations recorded in a darkroom when people enter it. Not only did they measure a slight increase in light intensity when people of normal disposition were in the room, they also noted a light

reduction if a person who is depressed or exhausted is in the room. The significance of this is huge as it suggests an active energy field that interacts with its environment sucking energy inwards as well as projecting it outwards.

Compounding the evidence for light emanation from the HEF, in 1988 Dr. Valerie Hunt measured the millivoltage signals projected from the body during a hands-on body manipulation process called Rolfing. In *'A Study of Structural Neuromuscular Energy Field and Emotional Approaches'*, she and her UCLA colleagues describe how they set up sensitive detection devices to record the emissions while simultaneously recording the colors seen by sensitives, people claiming to be able to 'see' auras. In their study they found conclusive evidence that different signals were being transmitted electrically from the body in different places and that the sensitives were able to correctly match their visual color with the scientific equipment. Dr. Hunt said: *"Throughout the centuries in which sensitives have seen and described the auric emissions, this is the first objective electronic evidence of frequency, amplitude and time, which validates their subjective observation of color discharge."*

This really is just the tip of the scientific iceberg regarding the volumes of data that have been collected. There is much more but it will come as no surprise that much of it is hotly debated and refuted by scientists. Of course, there is quackery in the field of human wellness just as there is in all human belief, but this is not evidence enough to dismiss all claims of a different reality than one professed by scientific data. Indeed, the furor surrounding the human energy field today is not so different from at anytime in the past when new paradigms have challenged the old and been met by a barrage of disapproval from people whose reputations are invested in the status quo. Theories such as Copernicus' solar system, Darwin's evolution, Bohr and Heisenberg's quantum theory have all first challenged and eventually changed the way we think about our universe and each was initially met with a barrage of derision and dismissal from established voices. *"There is no likelihood man can ever tap the power of the atom,"* said Robert Millikan, 1923 Nobel Laureate in Physics. It is a natural human reaction to doubt what you do not wish or hope to see but each time new mind rafts attain a critical mass of acceptance, our entire species evolves to an expanded level of consciousness that could not be met from within the confines of the original paradigm. It is no coincidence that when we accept a transformational perception of the world outside, how we feel about our own self also transforms and we begin to see our place in it a little differently.

A Brief Overview of Energy Systems in the Human Body

A conflict of paradigms determines our interpretation of history too. Does ancient philosophy merely represent the unsophisticated fantasies of savage people seeking solace from their primordial fears, or does it offer us insight into a profound spiritual awareness that has been lost and demands rediscovery if we are to meet the predicament of our current reality?

A successful interpretation of past wisdom relies upon an honest intention and willingness to translate complex ideas into a modern perspective. If we find solace in what we learn, we should use it, if we do not, we should discard it. The key is entering the spiral of learning without conclusions already made. If our intention is to find excuses to dismiss ancient ideas as bogus and naïve, we will surely find ammunition aplenty but if we are truly seeking transformation, then we must be prepared to sever our link with mind rafts that no longer serve their purpose.

One of the great barriers to learning that we initially meet is a suspicion that the philosophies of India and China are actually religions. Western minds, in particular, have been jaded by their experience of religion, but we should not tar new experience of ancient wisdom with the same brush that we tar modern interpretations of ancient religions. Although the health systems we are going to look at are connected to Brahmanism and Taoism, they are not religious. They do not require faith in one God or another. They are ***spiritual*** for they only require the person to take responsibility for their own health and wellbeing. Just like any philosophy, any way of life, practice makes perfect. In this respect, one could say that we need to ***apply them religiously,*** not change our religion in order to apply them.

To truly grasp the philosophical premise of Eastern health systems we have to understand that thousands of years ago, when these systems were being developed, people naturally regarded both their personal spirituality and the spirit of their communities to be vital components in their state of wellbeing. In the West, this connection has disintegrated from our social structure, purpose and processes as spirituality and a sense of community have become increasingly absent ingredients of our i-go-based societies. In contrast, Eastern temples, ashrams and other spiritual centers have, to some extent, thankfully retained their role as great nexuses of social and spiritual nourishment vital to the wellbeing of people they serve in their communities. While Western minds may regard the secular state as being an essential facet of personal freedom, the oft-resulting belief in nothing but fact is no less a belief system than the Islamic state or communism and is no less a factor influencing choices either.

A strong community is built upon people whose commonalities bind them together. In any community, ancient or modern, its state of health isn't determined solely by what people do but ***how*** they do it. A community of people who face adversity in isolation from one another endures far more suffering than a community that faces the same adversity in unity because the social obligation to share, help out and protect the weaker members of that community is eroded and the fear of isolation and abandonment sets in. Now consider a modern European or American city, a product of economic necessity cobbled together by fractured communities and dissolving family structures. This expansion of these huge pseudo-communities places untold stress on the entire global society as they are founded without solidarity of purpose or common conviction other than that of our personal right to individuality and freedom to make money and spend it. In contrast, for millennia Asian health systems have recognized that all human suffering is derived from desire and aversion and that our communities, those people who support the connected mind rafts by which we live, can either expand desire and aversion through separation or contract them through an energetic commitment to support and provide basic needs for one another.

In a very real sense, our modern values define our health as well as reflect it. We have created toxic environments of stress, distrust and disrespect. The energy of our minds is mirrored back at us in the energy of our world and vice versa. Eastern systems of wellbeing are holistic because the people who created them knew that medicine is just one aspect of wellness and that sustainable physical health is dependent upon our awareness here and now. Unless we are sensitive to our own mind and the countless thoughts flowing through it, how can we begin to adapt its composition?

Thousands of years ago, people intimately understood the connection between their health and their way of life because their personal truth made no division between the two. The result was entire wellbeing philosophies that still serve their purpose today because the causes and conditions for health, wellbeing and contentment remain absolutely the same: energetic presence.

TCM and Chakras

There are two Eastern health systems that we are going to look at in this section because they both describe an energy system that is integral to our understanding of how mental and spiritual energy are translated into physical effects. The first is TCM and the second is the chakra energy system.

TCM originates over 5000 years ago and is based upon systems of nature. The human body and everything in nature, says TCM, is comprised of five elemental forces: wood, metal, fire, water and earth. Qigong, herbal therapy, acupressure, foods for healing and Chinese psychology, the five basic techniques of TCM, are designed as both a preventative and remedial health system and as a regimen of self-exploration. In modern terms, these five elements might be compared to a daily routine of yoga, a massage, a balanced nutritious diet, a homeopathic course of natural herbs and a session with a psychologist. This regimen would certainly not look out of place in a modern journal on healthy living, let alone in a daily routine that is 5000 years old.

One of the basic principles of TCM is ***qi***, which is loosely translated as meaning vital energy. Qi is both the life force of the body and the means by which organs communicate and interact within it. TCM assigns organs both a physical function and an energetic function and each is connected to the properties of one element. Organs can develop qi deficiency, qi stagnation or qi excess, which consequently affects physical health.

Qi travels along ***meridians*** in the body, which are energy pathways. TCM has identified a network of 12 major meridian channels, each related to a major organ, acting as conduits for qi in the same way that veins are conduits for blood. The practice of TCM is to live life in a way that promotes and encourages the smooth passage of qi along the meridians of the body in order that the organs receive the life force they require for the body to remain healthy. Acupuncture or acupressure is specifically designed to manipulate the meridian system to stimulate the passage of qi or remove blockages in order that harmony in the body can be restored. If qi stagnates or becomes blocked, physical problems begin to materialize. For example, headaches or stomachaches can be the initial symptoms of an energy build-up and if this energy stagnates for too long it can materialize as physical growths.

The chakra system hails from different philosophical roots to TCM but there are also remarkable similarities. The earliest known mention of chakras is found in the later Upanishads, which are a series of 108 Brahman scriptures forming part of the Vedas. These were committed to text over a thousand-year period in India from around 800BC. Today, the Upanishads are considered the heart of the Hindu faith and other practices such as yoga. The word 'Upanishad' literally means 'to sit near' which is a reference to how the lessons were once taught to the student sitting at the feet of their master. There is little doubt that the Upanishads were once closely guarded secrets to which only the initiated were privy, as they were believed to bestow practitioners with the power of Gods.

The word 'chakra' has its origins in the Sanskrit word 'cakra', meaning 'wheel'. The wheel to which it refers is believed to be the wheel of life, the cycle of life and birth; however, it also refers to the physical nature of the chakras, which are the body's spinning energy centers. The human body has seven principle chakras, four secondary chakras, one etheric chakra, eight minor chakras, and hundreds of lesser chakras that act as energy centers, each associated with organs, glands and other physical matter in the body. They are purported to be the connection between the physical and the etheric or non-physical. When the chakras are functioning with enough vital energy, the body will be well, but if the energy flow is affected the vitality of the chakras is affected too and can even cause them to stop spinning and shut down altogether. This would be a symptom of physical problems soon to emerge.

The seven major chakras all have connections to physical, mental and spiritual functions. They are aligned along the spine from the root chakra on the tailbone to the crown chakra at the top of the head. In this system, the energy that feeds chakras and maintains their functions is called 'prana'. It serves a similar function to qi in TCM. Prana feeds the body with life force and is contained within the breath. According to chakra theory, breath is not just a means of supplying oxygen to the body but a vessel for carrying prana, the essential energy of the universe that all living beings require to function effectively. In India and all over Asia a vast number of meditative practices are focused on awareness of breathing which is said to have been the mechanism by which the Buddha achieved enlightenment. Such is the level of awareness that can be achieved by this technique and the familiarity with prana the practitioner can attain, it is said that a learned practitioner can know of their own death six months prior to it, because at this time prana no longer enters the body on the breath but leaves it, surplus to requirements for a body that is breaking down. Chakras are all fed by 72,000 energy channels called 'nadis' that run throughout the body, performing a very similar function to the meridians in TCM.

What is crucial to appreciate is what these energy systems imply. What was the purpose and motivation of ancient civilizations in mapping human energy so thoroughly, understanding it so intimately and building entire life-shaping methodologies around it? It seems a lot of effort just based upon conjecture. Were ancient practitioners merely seeking good health or was there some deeper spiritual imperative that is often lost in translation between the paradigms of history and the 21st century?

The reasons become clearer as we focus on two energy conduits in particular, detailed in both Chinese and Indian systems, known as ***ida and pingala*** nadis in the chakra system. Surprisingly, these nadis are immortalized in the caduceus, a symbol that represents Western allopathic medicine. Although the historical reason for why this symbol came to represent medicine seems to derive from a mistake in USA army iconography, we are learning that perhaps the synchronicity of events can extend to symbols spanning time to connect with concepts that they do indeed represent. Speculation perhaps, but that seems consistent with the nature of chaos.

As with the caduceus, the ida and pingala serpents spiral around a central spine. In chakra theory, this represents the yin-yang or male/female energies flowing through the chakras. If you recall, Count Von Reichenbach claimed to have detected this positive and negative charge related to the right and left sides of the human body respectively. In India the snake represents ***kundalini***, the energy that is purported to awaken when the ida and pingala nadis are fully opened and the chakras operating at optimum strength. Practices like qigong and yoga are specifically designed to remove blockages and stimulate the awakening of this energy as it is believed to elevate the human body to a higher or more refined state of energy related to the evolution of human consciousness.

Thus, TCM and chakra theory and the connected practices are energetic stimulants designed to elevate the energy from the base of the spine where the serpent sleeps, to the head that connects us to our higher spiritual purpose. To some people, this purpose would be called 'God'. It is noteworthy that the snake in Christian beliefs is the symbol of temptation or the Devil that led to the fall of man from the Garden of Eden. If we take the concept of kundalini energy (male and female united) and impose Adam and Eve in their place, what happens to the biblical story? Eve became tempted by desire and ate the apple causing humanity to be cast out from Paradise: the ***fall*** of humankind. Is it coincidental that kundalini energy, when fully awakened and its channels fully opened, is purported to be the means by which spiritual awakening or nirvana can be achieved? Perhaps the story of Adam and Eve represents how our obsession with the physical spiral of suffering, represented by the apple, commutes our energetic vibration (Adam and Eva or Ida and Pingala) to the physical plane and holds us here. Speculation it may be, but all the players in the Biblical story, even the basic concepts, are present and accounted for in its spiritual interpretation. The current challenge of humanity, i-go vs. spirit, is strikingly similar to the choice of remaining rooted in i-go or finding ways to experiment with our spiritual nature and elevate our spiritual energy. It is not inconceivable that, at some distant point in the history of human evolution, the ida and pingala energy systems were once united within our species only for our mental attachments to the physical world to split them apart and break our connection to a higher spiritual purpose. This interpretation is consistent with how our i-go's obsessions have attached our minds to the physical while closing off many of us to the spiritual aspects of ourselves. It is the fall of humankind on an entirely different level.

Once more we are reminded of the great difference in purpose between Eastern and allopathic medicine. While Western medicine has taken the physical route to health, seeking to prolong life and remove sickness, Eastern traditions perceive wellness as a byproduct of the journey towards an awakened mind, body and spirit. The body is perceived as the vehicle by which consciousness can assume a physical journey towards a higher state of being and if we are not in some way connected to that purpose through consciousness, awareness and sensitivity to the mental, energetic and spiritual signposts, the resulting ignorance of our own suffering results in a cry for help from our physical being. This cry is called 'sickness'.

From Energy into Matter

In 1970, Dr. Robert Ader and his colleagues in the department of psychiatry at the University of Rochester, New York, were experimenting with lab rats by giving them saccharine and synchronizing its ingestion with drug injections that caused the rats an upset stomach. The rats very quickly learned to avoid the saccharine. However, when conducting the experiment again without the injections, many of the rats still died from eating the saccharine. Ader realized that he had conditioned the rats' immune systems into a reflexive response. Very simply, their minds associated the saccharine with the stomach problems that triggered an automatic failure in their immune system. Ader's experiments were the first experimental proof that the mind and the body were inextricably linked. Rats could ***believe*** themselves to death!

In the 1990's Dr. Candice Pert, a neurobiologist, researcher and professor of Physiology and Biophysics at Georgetown University Medical Center, USA, began to piece together why such a phenomenon occurs in rats in a historical breakthrough in human beings. Pert identified the receptors for peptides within the human body. Peptides are the body's opiates, short chains of amino acids that communicate emotional information throughout the body. As emotions arise within your body, peptides that mirror the emotion are released from glands and attach themselves to your organs, endocrine glands, skin, muscle and other body tissues, storing emotional information like little chemical libraries. This amazing discovery once again shook the traditional understanding of how the mind-body connection works. Before this breakthrough, it was assumed that the mind was responsible for most emotional communication and all emotional memories were mental; but in discovering the receptors for peptides in virtually every place in the human body, Dr. Pert realized that emotions reside in the body too, as part of the living tissue of every human being. In other words, your body ***becomes*** your emotions. It is as much your emotional memory as your mind is.

The implications of this are staggering for us all. As events occur in your life, peptides reflecting your emotions are signaled for release into your body by your brain, literally recreating the event in your physical being. These peptides connect with receptors in the cells of your body, which act like communicators to the peptide secreting glands and cells. The amount and extent of peptides released relates to the frequency and duration of your feeling and each feeling seems to be connected to a particular organ or area of the body just as TCM and other Eastern methodologies have believed for millennia. Western medical science has now accumulated substantial evidence supporting the emotional-organ relationship to a far greater extent than a vast majority of practitioners would ever have given credence just a couple of decades ago. Fear, anger, frustration or bitterness really do have a long-term effect on the body. If we do not release these emotions, they can permanently damage our organs.

An Emotion Map of the Organs

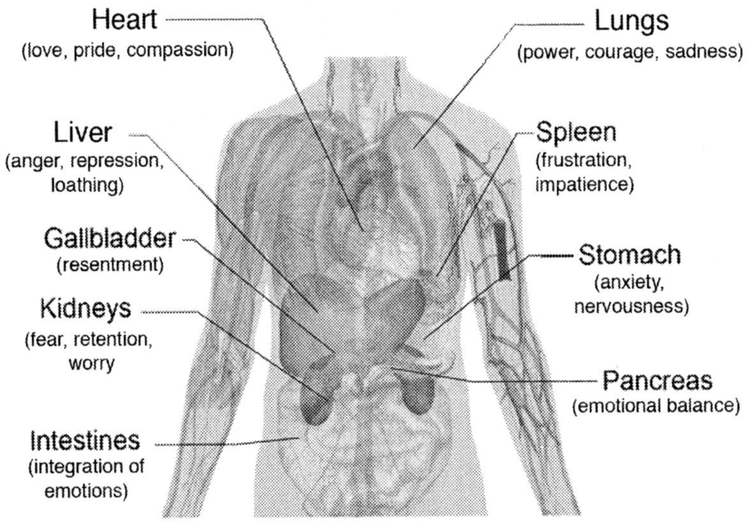

The anatomical charts of traditional Chinese medicine actually assign organs an emotional function as well as a physical function. Physical complications in that organ can indicate the underlying emotional causes of the physical complaint. For instance the lungs hold our sorrow, our liver our anger, our heart our love or hatred. If we hold onto these emotional states and fail to release their energy, it will reveal itself in those organs as the cause of more palpable physical sickness or disease. Western science has only recently conceded that the root causes of some physical symptoms can be found in emotional states, particularly stress or fear. A stressed stomach, for example, is known to increase the likelihood of ulcers, certain cancers are also being shown to be stress-related and it has been discovered that stressed organs have deteriorated tissue and can result in mutated cells. It may not be long before Western medicine 'discovers' that emotions are a causal factor in all disease and sickness, it is just a matter of 'proving' it for people to begin believing it.

Seemingly, everything in our reality affects us. Nothing is neutral because everything has 'energetic presence' in our lives. Every thought, every word, every action, every emotion, every physical object, everything to which we give presence in our reality is reflected in our mind, our physical body and our spirit. There is plenty of evidence piling up. Indeed, the effects of these conditions have been shown in a bewildering and growing multitude of experiments, which individually could be dismissed as being anomalous but in their totality give us further insight into the depth of evidence connecting our state of our wellbeing with our state of health.

- Scientists claim a strong link between loneliness and Alzheimer's disease. Researchers at the Rush University Medical Center in Chicago studied 823 people over a four-year period with an average age of approximately 81 years. Participants were assessed for loneliness and given a score on a scale of 1-5. Researchers found that every point of loneliness was equivalent to a 51 per cent increase in the chances of developing Alzheimer's disease.[6]
- An experiment in the New England Journal of Medicine reported that we become more susceptible to sickness after experiencing something in our life we perceive as being negative.[7]
- The Journal of the American Medical Association reported a similar experiment that found people without strong

social connections were four times more likely to develop the symptoms of a cold than people with a greater variety of friends.[8]

- In a study conducted in Finland, 96,000 health records of widowed people were studied and showed that the probability of death doubled in the week after being widowed.[9]
- Another study in Finland tested 2428 men aged 42 to 60 years for the feeling of helplessness. Six years later these men were tested again and the study discovered that those men with high helplessness scores were 3.4 times more likely to have died than those with lower scores. In fact, having excluded medical conditions that already existed in those men, the likelihood of death of those feeling most helpless was six times higher than the empowered men.[10]
- In a 1995 article in the medical journal Lancet, Dr. Kiecolt-Glaser compared the speed of wounds healing between empowered people and people who had been in the long-term situation of caring for a sick relative and therefore felt helpless to affect their reality. The experiment showed that after six weeks, 55 per cent of the empowered people's wounds were healed compared to only 17 per cent for the others.[11]

These examples are just a glimpse of a vast array of evidence supporting the connection between how we feel about our life and the physical health of our body. You possess the personal power to manifest sickness or wellbeing. The whole idea that reality is entirely objective and measurable is preposterous when we accept that our subjective feelings are the primary force shaping it into who we are and what it is. Your entire body of experience, emotion and belief, your complete identity, is brought to bear on your reality at every moment of every day.

One part of your life reflects the next, just as your mind reflects your body, your body reflects your spirit and your spirit reflects your mind. In other words, if you are getting sick, what are you thinking? What are you feeling? What mind rafts are supporting the presence of sickness in your life? What historical feelings might still be clinging to your cells? And, if you are not sick, what do you need to do to ensure that you stay that way? Are you dealing with your emotions maturely, or suppressing or holding onto them as if they were 'me' and 'mine'?

Eastern philosophies ooze belief in the spirituality of humanity. Being of a scientific nature, Western allopathic medicine entirely rejects any such idea as nonsense. This places the onus for our health on the initiated doctors and specialists who diagnose us, fix us and then rediagnose and refix us when it all goes wrong again. The problem with this technique is that nothing is going wrong and there is nothing to fix.

Our physical health is not a medical problem. It is a spiritual-energetic problem. It always has been and always will be no matter how much we cut, chop, manage and cure our physical symptoms. Physical intervention becomes necessary in many cases because the causes of sickness are not detected at an early stage through our self-awareness. While we do not suspect that the causes are our own self, this trend is set to continue. Thus, it is a fair claim to make that the primary cause of dis-ease, of being ill at ease in the physical realm, is ***ignorance of self***. While diet and exercise defines aspects of your physicality, the manner in which you eat and take care of your physical body reflects more profound values such as the state of your relationship with your own self. Do you love yourself? Are you conscious of who you are, what you are eating and how you are moving? Do you want to be well or do you subconsciously need to be sick to give your life meaning? The ultimate underlying cause of all these questions is how well you know your own self: sensitivity. The questions are answered in full only when you begin to perceive physical health, not through the crude filter of fear of sickness and dying, but through the deepest comprehension that your physical body is an energetic vessel to carry you onward through life and upward through the energetic vibration that we are all destined to explore.

Eastern methodologies have not lost sight of this purpose. They embrace it. They empower people to act. They bring action to faith and method to theory. They offer the means for all people to be healthy, to be well, but also to rise above the fear and self-loathing that plagues Western philosophical approaches to health and damns so many of us to a meaningless physical reality that can never serve the purpose of joy and contentment. When we begin to see life as an energetic journey and not a material one, then reality changes and so does our relationship to physical health and our awareness of its part in energetic creativity.

Allopathy disempowers and removes responsibility from the individual. Good wellness systems empower each of us to seek awareness through an honest and frank assessment of who we are and what we mean before wellbeing is achievable. Driven by self, by i-go and by the 'I', 'me' and 'mine' culture that runs rampant through capitalist consumerism, we are achieving reduction of self but only on the level of physical self-destruction, not through the awareness of our truest spiritual identity. We destroy the body through ignorance, through a fear of asking what it really is and why we have been blessed with a body in the first place. We do not wish to enquire as to these real reasons because the answer shatters the illusion upon which the most fundamental mind rafts of our reality is founded. Vladimir Lenin understood the nature of lies and said knowingly: *"A lie told often enough becomes the truth."* Many of us are consummate liars to our own self and society applauds and rewards these lies with the material gains that further shroud who we are and what we mean. We hold up material winners as models for us all and perpetuate the suffering they hide with wealth. We can continue believing that this little clod of flesh, bone, beliefs and assumptions that we think we are is the ultimate reality that we seek, or we can begin to deconstruct the fantasy that starts with the illusion of self.

If you build a reality that begins inside of you rather than trying to match the inside with what you see going on outside, you will reveal the true nature of both. Awareness builds this. It also builds health and wellbeing. Ignorance of your own ignorance is a quandary that mires the mind in the routines and patterns that have created all your problems. Questions in your mind become impossible to answer when the answers are concealed within a paradigm of thinking that you have excluded from your reality. Living disconnected from your own self, disconnected from your body, disconnected from your state of mind, you disconnect from the energies that nurture your physical, mental, energetic and spiritual forms. Thus you get sick. Physical, mental, energetic, spiritual sickness all hail from ignorance and all ignorance hails from your failure to connect with your own self.

It is time to evolve beyond 'I' and wonder what is in it for 'we'.

Part II: Provolution of Spirit

Chapter 8

Spiritual Power

"Our scientific power has outrun our spiritual power. We have guided missiles and misguided men."
Martin Luther King Jr. – American Civil Rights Leader
(1929 - 1968)

The Yin-Yang I-go

In Part I of Provolution we looked at how you are a product of i-go-based mind rafts that translate into energy systems causing replication physically, mentally and spiritually across uni-time. In Part II we are going to place your i-go in the bigger picture connected to the u-go's and we-go's with whom you share this planet and contextualize this within the awesome mechanisms of the universe as a whole. We will also be asking how we apply the new mind rafts we have learned in the first part of Provolution to connect to people on a spiritual level while fulfilling the very practical needs in all human lives.

Whether engaged in material or spiritual pursuits, every consciousness on earth is i-go-based to some extent or another. The strange irony is that even when we are in the process of liberating ourselves from i-go, we are still driven by it, however spiritual and selfless our motives might be. I-go offers our awareness a great source of purpose if we can learn to evolve it consciously and conscientiously. It is a strange quirk of this universe that the only way for i-go to disappear is for it to destroy itself through total awareness of what it is and how it works. Thus, i-go is not only responsible for ***creating*** 'you' in your current form, it will also be responsible for the choice to ***destroy*** 'you', by which I mean the mind raft of self that has convinced you of the separateness and independence of your existence.

This strange dualism is exactly what we have come to expect from a paradoxical yin-yang universe and while it may be somewhat confusing, we should be getting used to the fact that the universe wasn't made merely for the purpose of our left brain to understand it. While i-go often distorts our impression of the world into believing that things are divided into black and white stereotypes, this is a very misleading oversimplification because i-go is also responsible for the infinite variety of personalities in the world. No two people are the same and this is because i-go has an infinite range of possible expressions, some hard, some soft, some imposing, some accommodating. Sometimes we come face to face with the strongest i-go's without even knowing that it is i-go that we are facing. This is i-go's deceptive nature. In this chapter we are going to depict its two faces by unmasking the yin-yang aspects that reside inside us all and asking which dominate our behavior. By seeing ***all*** action in terms of i-go, we can ask, "What's the alternative and how do we cultivate it?" Between yin and yang i-go, what choice do we have?

Just like the yin-yang, i-go can be strong, it can be weak, it can be resilient, it can yield, it can grow and it can ebb, all dependent upon your feelings at any given moment. In different situations, you will react in different i-go modes depending on the predominant mind rafts you have learned in your life. Some of us have learned to be predominantly yin (female) and some of us have learned to be predominantly yang (male). As you will see, these predispositions do not necessarily divide along sexual lines but according to our self-perception and the way we relate to the world around us. There are plenty of yin men in the world and equally plenty of yang women. While male i-go may seem harder or stronger, it still has a soft aspect just as the softer female aspect has strong aspects too. Once again, these seemingly opposing forces have opposites within them, giving rise to the complex personalities of human beings comprised of flowing and interchanging strengths and weaknesses. If you expand awareness of these traits in real time you can begin to identify aspects of yourself that are in excess and causing you suffering. You can then take steps to shift the excess back towards a more harmonious balance between the two.

The yang i-go is outwardly domineering and control-centered but this is just half of its story. While yang i-go can be boastful, proud and narcissistic driving your anger, your frustration and your need to be recognized by others, it also gives rise to tenacity, hard work, the motivation to fight, and to be resilient or rebellious. In general, yang i-go is focused on the outward appearance of things, demanding to be in control and that others recognize, celebrate and concur with its needs. But it is also a prerequisite of our ability to persevere with goals and ambitions, to take heart in hard times and to believe in projects that are not yet physically complete. Without yang i-go driving us forwards it would be difficult to get things done.

The yin aspect of i-go is the softer, female facet of yourself. It is flexible and accepting, gracious and inclusive, yielding and supple, soft and inclusive but, just like yang i-go, when we pour too much energy into it, an imbalance occurs that is disturbingly prevalent in modern society. Excess yin i-go gives rise to the false humility and self-deprecation that fuels so many people's low self-esteem. This is the demon that nags you into believing that you are not good enough, don't deserve what you have or what you desire, and that you are too stupid, ugly, poor, weak, slow, (you fill in the adjective of choice) to achieve anything worthwhile. It expects failure; indeed it self-sabotages success, rejects praise and believes in its own inadequacies to such an extent that they materialize as reality.

But we must temper our impression of yin i-go by remembering that the female aspect of all people is also that which finds moderation, yields and seeks harmony in conflict. It is why women have such wonderful patience and acceptance while men tend to be more impatient and demanding. Of course, these are generalizations and tendencies as all of us will operate in both modes at some point today whatever physical sex we are.

Excess Yin I-go	**Harmonious Human Spirit**	**Excess Yang I-go**
Shy	Self-Confident	Arrogant
Indecisive	Decisive	Dictatorial
Assumptive	Analytical	Argumentative
Naive	Inquisitive	Critical
Repressed	Empathetic	Needy
Reclusive	Bonds Well	Manipulative
Sanctimonious	Sensitive	Hedonistic
Unfocused	Determined	Fanatical
Fearful	Strategic	Controlling
Amoral	Consistent	Hypocritical
Conforming	Challenge-Seeking	Fantasizing
Faithless	Spiritual	Zealous
Undiscerning	Impartial	Prejudiced
Vulnerable	Confident	Arrogant
Disorderedly	Graceful	Ostentatious
Secretive	Transparent	Gullible
Alienating	Accepting	Doting
Easily Bored	Uses Free Time Creatively	Wastes Time
Skeptical	Faithful	Whimsical
Ineffective	Constructive	Impractical

The chart above outlines the two excesses of i-go joined together by their harmonious aspect: human spirit. We all have a predominant side, either yin or yang, and both are as powerful as one another, despite yang appearing the stronger. Yang provides us with the stereotypical i-go in the form of the self-loving, control-seeking narcissist but we do not always perceive the shy yin aspect requiring the same measure of power to exist, but it does indeed. In suicidal people, their sense of utter worthlessness and despair is so profound and their i-go associates with the negative self-perception they have generated so strongly that they exhibit its destructive power through repetitive thoughts of low self-worth or self-loathing. None of this is any less of a delusion than the pride and preening of the yang i-go, of course, but this merely illustrates the tendency of i-go to exaggerate all feelings to an extreme if we do not observe them in awareness and with a sense of proportion.

I-go is a complex creation of your reactive self, swinging moods and emotions from yin to yang throughout your day. We will be looking more comprehensively at human spirit in a later chapter but I introduce it here to demonstrate its composition as a harmonious confluence of yin and yang in the very same way that the present is the meeting of the past and the future. Human spirit is the self-aware and sensitive aspect of yourself that is not to be created within you, but to be discovered. When you participate and cling to your emotions as 'I', 'me' and 'mine' you suspend them in their growth and maturity phase of their life cycle, thus storing the emotional energy in your mind and body and anchoring your future to events that will reincarnate your emotional attachments for as long as you energetically cling to them.

I define spirituality as getting to know your 'self' and one of the most powerful techniques you can learn in life is familiarizing yourself with how you react to events. Observing your reactions is a profoundly spiritual process because mastering the technique requires that you become intimately engaged and aware of your inner space in order to catch a reaction as it occurs and observe it without judgment, i-go or adding to the emotional fuel within you. You cannot observe yourself if you are not aware of your mind, your thoughts and your feelings as they arise.

Conversely, reacting to events is an i-go-based process because it happens in non-awareness, without mindfulness. As soon as your i-go springs into action, it launches your reactive mode and your conditioned yin-yang bias launches the connected i-go mind rafts to justify, rationalize, argue and condemn what is going on around you. This guarantees the repetition of emotional events because you will have no awareness of why you feel the way you do or how to stop the feeling expanding in the future. When a situation might require self-confidence for example, the harmonious spiritual reaction to the event, i-go-based arrogance or shyness might surface in unconscious reaction because that is the predominant mind raft you have carried around with you all your life. And practice makes perfect.

Look down the i-go chart again and analyze your own predominant reactions. Are you a yin or yang reactor? Whichever you are, observation in spirit mode will get you better results every time because it removes the sense of 'I', 'me' and 'mine' from your choice. However, how do you stop the spiral of reaction and generate observation? How do you stop becoming and start being? These questions have been the staple of spiritual practice for millennia because the key to spirituality is not about being holy, pure or having a great ponytail. It is about reconditioning your mind from being primed to react to its learning and to become a mind that knows nothing and observes everything.

Calming I-go

Each of us is born into the world with a challenge to see things for how they are, not as they seem and this challenge begins and ends with you. I-go is not reality. It is the distortion that confounds your appreciation of it. How can you join the dots of life through a filter of permanence and division, through fear and threat, through avoidance and shame, when these are reactions to reality, not deep appreciation of it? Take a few moments to sit and listen to your own mind, to analyze the forces at play within the space you call yourself and you will surely discover your i-go at the root of everything you create in no time at all. When you do this you will also discover that a reality viewed through i-go is a shape-shifting distortion, not a profound revelation.

Johann Georg Ritter von Zimmermann, the Swiss philosopher said: *"...no one can be truly great until he has gained a knowledge of himself, a knowledge which can only be acquired by occasional retirement."* I-go expands in this world because billions passionately practice its daily expansion, while contraction is a specialized discipline reserved for mystics and aesthetics. This perception is rapidly changing, however, as the burgeoning spiritual section of your local bookstore will attest to. However, contracting i-go and embracing spirituality require a degree of focused introspection that can appear both extreme and absurd to minds conditioned to find satisfaction in transient physical pleasures. While 99 per cent of humanity accepts the conventional version of who they are and what they mean, the search for alternative meaning does not always seem rational. Why pursue alternatives when it is clear that the meaning of life is to be more beautiful, to own a new sports car, to have a highly paid job, to get a university degree; to do all those things that reinforce an illusory sense of self at the expense of your emotional and energetic freedom? This is the ultimate i-go trap.

When you are stuck in prison, a prison break does not seem so extreme, does it? It only seems extreme to the captors on the outside who fear the crazy people inside. If you are to liberate yourself from the squatter in your mind, your life-changing practice must actually involve a change in your life. A commitment to personal provolution, to a positive personal expansion of awareness that takes back the personal power you have to create something joyful, pleasant and peaceful in your reality, will take faith, a shock to your system, an evolution of behavior that propels you into a new paradigm. You cannot expect to change by clinging onto everything that you already have. While the very idea of provolution to someone locked away in a permanent world of suffering can seem bizarre, threatening and radical, there is nothing more radical than accepting the suffering you currently endure as if it is normal.

One of the greatest obstacles to your provolution is the fear of tribal rejection that arises when you consider the consequences of acting in discernibly different ways from the people around you. If you focus on this, the fear can become so pervasive that you will simply procrastinate and not actually ***do*** anything different. Yet, provolution is about you and it is time to start doing things ***for*** you, not out of selfishness but out of self-love.

People ask me if spirituality really needs to be as extreme as a committed regular practice. No, it doesn't but it depends what you want to achieve. If you want to be fit you have to jog regularly or go to the gym. If you want to have a healthy diet, you have to balance what you eat and be aware of the nutritional contents of each meal. If you want to pass an exam, you have to study hard. I do not perceive a regular spiritual practice as any more extreme or radical than practicing or learning about anything that you want to do well or be good at. Therefore it makes sense that if you want to be good at living, you have to study the laws of life and if you want to be great at it, you have to study hard. It is just doing what is necessary to create real and profound change in your life.

Is it really so extreme to practice a daily routine of meditation lasting 20-30 minutes? Is it really so radical to learn Tai Chi and raise your awareness of your mind/body relationship that you have separated and divided from one another? Is it really so bizarre to take a 10 day retreat and explore the i-go that defines your perception of yourself and your world? Is it really so drastic to discard the mind rafts of competition and conflict and seek a middle way of cooperation and unity in your community? Is it really so fanatical to ***expect*** and ***demand*** this time with yourself on a daily basis, without question, without compromise? Of course it is not. This is the kind of knowledge and retirement that Zimmermann was prescribing. It should be no more radical in a life seeking peace than it is to brush your teeth in a life seeking good personal hygiene. Provolution requires a different regime in your life than the old habit-inducing formula that has got you this far. The same tired solutions to the same old problems will only repeat and reinforce suffering that has become habitual.

A meditative practice might seem strange to you if you have never tried one but consider this: meditation is spiritual medicine in the same way that drugs are physical medicine. If you are to advance to a successful spiritual cure for your problems in life you should first explore and familiarize yourself with every cause, shouldn't you? The more information and experience you acquire regarding the root problems, the more likely you are to cure them for good. Your cycle of suffering begins and ends in ignorance of your i-go's behavior. Thus the solution is undertaking a practice that fosters as much awareness of it as you can possibly muster. Like pharmaceuticals, spiritual medicine may not always taste sweet, but it gets the job done.

It is a common complaint of meditators that meditation is impossible because they cannot concentrate. I always ask, "What happens when you meditate?" and they reply that "A million thoughts go around in my head. It is so frustrating. Meditation doesn't work for me!" But what they are really experiencing is the huge frustration of a mind out of control: a reactive, i-go-based mind that is controlling them when they believe that the opposite must be true. If you close your eyes for five minutes and concentrate on your breath as it enters and leaves your nose, you will quickly discover your attention digressing towards the latest mental news flashes regarding your next meeting, the recent argument you had with your spouse, a song revolving in your head, how hungry you are, the itchy leg that you just have to scratch; the mind processes a multitude of distractions that pile up and confound the peace you expect to find. When you experience this for the first time you think that you must be meditating wrongly or it doesn't work. "Isn't meditation supposed to be peaceful?" you may ask. Yet it is absurd that we expect to spend our entire life compelled to react and respond by an obsessive mind and then, in three minutes, achieve total peace and quiet! We have to set our goals a little more realistically and understand what meditation can achieve and what it cannot.

Not unlike an unruly child who has been spoiled, the brattish behavior of the i-go mind will not be undone by five minutes of close attention. It will take time, love, a hard lesson or two and a lot of hard work to observe the mind in action before you can create a mind at rest. The first step to doing this is to get to know the child, get to know your mind, get to know the conditions that you have created and desire to un-create. If you live 12 hours a day from within i-go, 20 minutes spent in awareness of it is not such an extreme practice, is it?

The saying goes that in the kingdom of the blind the one-eyed man is king and it is similar in the kingdom of i-go. The difference is that the i-go's blindness is curable, not by transplant, not by drugs, not even by hacking it out. To be king of your i-go all you need is a little awareness that it exists and faith that the only cure you need is awareness of yourself. This insight alone offers you the choice to be ignorant no longer and begin a journey towards the ultimate revelation of exactly what your true self really is.

Chapter 9

Death and Rebirth

"You will always exist in the universe in one form or another."
Shunryu Suzuki Roshi, Soto Zen Priest (1905 - 1971)

Recycling Parts

There are two types of people in this world: those who believe in a recycled spirit and those who do not. This choice determines some of the most profound answers you find in life, thus the questions you ask and directions that you choose to take while alive. In this section we are going to examine where we have acquired our mind rafts of death and enquire into the perception of mortality within Western religions. We will compare common religious views with the natural patterns that could or should influence our perception of this incredible natural transformation and reinforce the principle that no mind rafts serve you if they are the source of your suffering. In this section you have the opportunity to transform the fear and threat that shrouds your view of death into an opportunity for provolution in your view of life.

Just as we separate one object or person from another, so we separate life from death too. Some people assume that physical death is a permanent, absolute boundary between one state of existence and another because the same limits of imagination and experience seem to bring order to other areas of our existence. Death must be absolute, we tell ourselves, because the body rots away and we can find no empirical evidence that a soul or spirit endures beyond it. But perhaps we are just looking for evidence in all the wrong places?

Wikipedia says this about classifying what is alive and what is not:

> *"There is no universal definition of life.* ***To define life in unequivocal terms is still a challenge for scientists****, as the definition must be sufficiently broad that would encompass all life with which we are familiar. It should be sufficiently general that, with it, scientists would not miss life that may be* ***fundamentally different from earthly life****."* (my emphasis)

So what are we trying to define when we say something is 'alive' considering that we must include in that definition those life forms that may be fundamentally different from earthly life? It is not such an easy task to include everything that is not known now, is it? Perhaps by 'fundamentally different' we should review why the animate and inanimate are considered so fundamentally opposed in the first place and question whether those things we define as non-living are really as dead as they seem.

All life is made from the same energetic components. Science classifies something as living when those components have organized themselves into particular systems or characteristics such as homeostasis, metabolism, growth, adaptation, response to stimuli, reproduction etc, but these are otherwise arbitrary scientific classifications that group things together while also dividing one thing from another. Nature does not care about human distinctions. In reality, everything from a star to a clod of earth is still an aggregate of various energy forms collected together into different shapes and sizes. 'Life' is just a word with a meaning that people have ascribed to it and because people consider themselves living, the word has taken on a mystical, almost religious connotation that is worthy of division from all things that are not. We simply cannot understand how aggregates can form into such complex organizations that they spontaneously begin to do such inexplicable things as move, think, choose, speak, procreate and interact with the world in so many ways that there must surely be something inherently different between a 'living' organism and the 'dead' parts from which it is made.

In fact, the words 'animate' and 'inanimate' merely describe how matter interacts with its surroundings: actively or passively. While living beings affect change through both active and passive choice, non-living objects relate to their environment only passively, through the properties that they hold at any given moment. By this I mean that a cat goes about its life making choices to walk through grass, hunt birds, scratch its claws down trees and hiss at dogs. It actively ***chooses*** to hiss at dogs and scratch trees but by walking through grass it also passively affects its environment in ways that are by-products of its choice, such as by breaking grass stems or crushing insects as it makes its way through the grass. A cat actively relates to its environment in a way that a rock cannot. Still, this does not mean a rock has no effect at all. While a rock on a beach may not actively choose to affect the water that crashes against it, it affects the water regardless.

My point is not to dispute the designation of life per se, nor to get into a game of semantics about what is living or not. I am really concerned with the way in which our classifications of life and death imply a permanent condition, when nothing exists in a permanent condition. In this way we obscure the connections that bind all matter together in one gigantic series of on-going interactions and forget that 'dead' matter is destined to become living matter and living matter destined to become dead matter. From this false premise we extrapolate all sorts of misleading conclusions about life and death when the difference between the two seems as much a matter of perspective on a universal scale of time as anything else. While the rock appears inanimate today because it does not have the ability to procreate or a central nervous system, not only is it already a part of such a system in uni-time, from a global perspective it is already part of the earth's living system now, isn't it? Like a dead hair on your scalp, so a rock sits on the top of a mountain experiencing the process of transience in its own unique fashion.

If life is a dubious concept, then its partner, death, is no less flawed. Like yin-yang energy, everything we call life today is actually a composite of both life and death. They exist simultaneously, reliant upon one another and thus anything in the process of 'life' is also in the process of 'death'. Where does the process begin and end when they give rise to one another? Within you this paradox occurs in every cell of your body, through your regenerating organs to your skin, your hair, your blood, the oxygen flowing through your body, each flowing from expansion to contraction and back again in an endless series of expansions and contractions, connections and disconnections. We are all living and dying at the same time. So what is the driving instinct compelling us to differentiate between the two at all?

Organized Religion

Despite its purpose, organized religion does no better job than science at defining the transition from physical life to physical death. This is due to the same problem that all religions face, Western or otherwise. Jiddu Krishnamurti, the Master Teacher of the Order of the Star, told a story that perfectly illustrates this view in the Netherlands in August 1929 as he disbanded the very sect that had been initiated to follow him. He said:

> *You may remember the story of how the devil and a friend of his were walking down the street, when they saw ahead of them a man stoop down and pick up something from the ground, look at it, and put it away in his pocket. The friend said to the devil, 'What did that man pick up?' 'He picked up a piece of the truth,' said the devil. 'That is a very bad business for you, then,' said his friend. 'Oh, not at all,' the devil replied, 'I am going to help him organize it.'*
>
> *"I maintain that truth is a pathless land, and you cannot*

> *approach it by any path whatsoever, by any religion, by any sect. That is my point of view, and I adhere to that absolutely and unconditionally. Truth, being limitless, unconditioned, unapproachable by any path whatsoever, cannot be organized; nor should any organization be formed to lead or coerce people along a particular path.*

Identifying religions as ***organized systems*** is enlightening for it clearly reveals the dangers inherent when interpreting other people's ideas. As you now know, you will always translate an idea through the filter of your own i-go. Even if the words are channeled from God Himself, the interpretation is distinctly yours, mine or that of any guru/priest/cleric/imam who receives them. If the teacher says, "love thy neighbor", I must interpret what my teacher means by 'love' and what he does not before I can teach it to anyone else and if my mind is not as evolved as the teacher's, my explanation cannot possibly be as evolved either. The teachings that I translate through my mind and organize according to its structures are more shaped by my personal limitations than by the teacher's intentions. Moreover, my social standing depends upon maintaining the perceived integrity and truth of my teachings so there is great i-go pressure for me to place all kinds of warnings and threats about what will happen if the truth I teach is not followed 'religiously' by my congregation. This is how the subtle nuances of a teacher's thoughts, words and actions are trimmed away, the meaning slimmed down and the sum of his/her life 'refined' into rules dividing right from wrong, truth from blasphemy, saintly from wicked.

Religions don't deal in the ambiguity of grays. They can find no truth in shades. The minds of organized religions were trained in the same i-go mind rafts as the rest of us are trained in today. They deal in the truth of truth because their claim to teach it depends upon there being only one. Think about this. According to the "World Christian Encyclopedia" there are 270 major religious groups in the world today,[12] each divided into smaller and smaller sub categories and sects. ***People*** build the divisions and the limits, not our gods and certainly not the enlightened teachers who came to ***live*** the light of truth, not to invent it. In a world where the largest religious sect, Christianity, has 2.1 billion members divided into ***34,000 separate denominations***, which one is right? Is this not the clearest sign of i-go at work, dividing and conflicting?

Religions have boiled down vast multi-dimensional spiritual themes into attractive and colorful rituals and have become obsessed by the words of the teachers and the books written about them, not ***by*** them, but the one thing that characterizes all the great teachers is that they asked people to ***live*** the truth, not just ***know*** it or ***believe*** it. What they said wasn't as important as what they ***did***. Although the spiritual teachers of the past spoke of habits and rituals, they did not pause their daily routine to practice them. Their daily routine ***was*** their practice. In short, the practice of the greatest spirits on this planet, in the past as today, is application of profound awareness from one breath to the next.

Conditioning Religious Views of Death

If we are to understand why we possess the perception of death that we do and adjust it so that it serves our purpose in life, we need to strip away the i-go that lies hidden at its heart. We have already established how the competitive mind rafts of i-go condition our social, economic and political systems; now we must ask whether our perception of physical death has been fashioned from the very same stuff and, if it has, what alternative mind rafts could we choose from?

I was brought up in the Church of England but have had the privilege to live and work in Islamic and Buddhist countries for many years. There is little doubt in my mind that the vast majority of religious orders are reflections of the i-go's that interpreted them and that their prevailing view of death is no less a creation of the same. This is not a slur on religions. Indeed, we should be surprised to find any religions that are ***not*** products of i-go considering its almost endemic expansion in the world. Yet the evidence is clear: the use of fear, shame, guilt, separation, limit and demand for obedience are unmistakable traits of i-go and they exist at the heart of the vast majority of religious orders, particularly Judeo-Christian. For example, Christianity, Judaism and Islam all claim that we are born sinful, live a single life and when we die, God Himself judges us. The righteous will enter Heaven and the non-righteous will go to Hell, so we are warned. Religious congregations are organized around a fear of death, judgment and potential for eternal damnation. Unless we are 'good', which is often a euphemism for 'doing what we are told by our religious leaders', we will be punished. The fear and control rife within these mind rafts are all obvious fingerprints of the i-go at work.

Fear is neither the tool of a loving God nor the device from which to construct a contented life. It resembles a weapon of humanity far more than an aspect of divinity. While you remain dependent upon an external clergy to answer the greatest questions in your life you will forever ignore the real answers awaiting discovery within you. What else in nature have you witnessed being born, dying and then stopping the transition? What precedence is there for it? Is it more likely, considering the evidence for interconnected and interdependent transience that you have read so far in this book, that everything ***except*** the notion of death is an illusion perpetrated by i-go or that it is more likely that the single life theory of many religions is in fact consistent with the illusion?

Religion presents people with an icon of death, a caricature that plays on the fears of the i-go. It is unrelated to the naturally transient process of life. While this is not the unique fault of religions but a global trend that they support and from which they derive their support, religions have a massive responsibility to challenge and test their truth with the greatest vigor. The compassion, love, forgiveness and charity personified by the most respected religious teachers must be ***practiced*** if it is to mean anything at all. It doesn't matter what you know, only what you act upon, and if religious congregations lived like their prophets, Jews wouldn't kill Muslims, Muslims wouldn't kill Christians and Christians wouldn't kill Jews.

If religions were truly applied, they would cease to be religions at all. They would quickly become transitory mind rafts constantly elevated by the higher and higher intentions of their practitioners. We could detach from the idea of truth and simply choose to nurture the awakening of more and more subtle layers of awareness within ourselves. In this way, humanity would be nurtured simply for the purpose of being worthy and in need of nurturing. Discard painful mind rafts. Absorb and adopt the beneficial and awe-inspiring. If we did this, rather than being stuck in the religious maelstrom of God's will, we could take full responsibility for the mess we have crafted from human will.

It is as though love, empathy, community, self-knowledge, piety and wisdom have been abandoned as impractical in a world where hatred, fear, threat and competition are the common currency. But we can change this. Instead of sitting around praying for external transformation, you can transform your understanding of life and death and adopt a new mind raft, which accepts that the most powerful prayer you have ever said has ***already*** been answered. It is the prayer to be born in a physical body, to be here and now and with the highest of intentions to create provolution in your own life.

If you conclude, as I have, that viewing life as a one-shot deal is incredibly unhelpful to your understanding of why you are here and what you mean, you can start placing physical death into the same context as life. It is time that you started releasing the fear-based reaction shrouding your perception of death and replace it with some mind rafts that help you to get better results in life here and now. It is time that you contextualized your human spirit in the interconnected and interdependent reality that lies beneath the physical surface. And it is time to include in your personal truth the ***possibility*** that we not only condition events in this life, but we also condition life after life and ***rebirth itself***. If you open your mind to this potentiality, nothing is impossible and things in life that were once mysterious begin to be revealed in greater and greater detail.

Conditioning Rebirth

Uni-time posits that you are a complete multidimensional map of everything you have ever experienced, energetically stored in your mind, body and spirit. Your past lives on inside you and to experience a different future, you must become someone different ***now***. That means changing your reaction to present events and ending the past conditions that gave rise to them. Every experience in the present moment provides you with a real-time opportunity to expand awareness of yourself in order to learn and change your future.

Most people go through life without a clue about what they are really doing, thinking, saying or feeling. They do not live in the present but are always planning, dreaming, hoping, remembering and thinking that the art of living requires as much awareness as driving or brushing their teeth. If you have learned to be an observer of the present, not a participator, you will have become comfortable in uni-time and no are longer sucked into the illusion of becoming rather than simply being. Once you master this skill through the awareness practice of your choice, each event becomes an opportunity where ***the future chooses you*** rather than grasping and clinging to a future you desperately desire or believe you need.

It may sound a little bit mad to believe that the future chooses you if you have been brought up in a thinking system that so fervently holds to the idea of free will, but that is because the conventional view perceives the universe as being an objective place or a three-dimensional object. This perception evolves if you begin to think of the universe as a living act of conscious creation, more a living and developing being than an object. The universe is like a huge lake in uni-time, connecting together molecule by molecule the infinite interdependent conditions that are being caused by i-go. The ripples of chemical, kinetic, mechanical and other energetic forces are playing out in its depths and were we to observe these forces without i-go it would be like watching a movie playing out in front of us. But, we choose to perceive i-go as being 'real' and thus become universal actors, writing our own script and stealing a scene or two for our personal desire. In effect, most people ***participate*** in the movie and spend their lives trying to supplant the natural evolution of the universe with the desires and aversions of their i-go. Only i-go could seriously believe that the entire universe should adapt its plan in order to accommodate the desires of 'me'.

This is what is meant by the future choosing you, not you choosing your future. The universe will play out every ripple you have ever created on the lake of uni-time because you have already conditioned them into your personal future and thus into the future of the universe. Rather than creating more, ***trying to fix what has not gone wrong,*** become an observer rather than a participator. If you do this, one day the conditions that you have created will end.

Now expand this concept outwards across time and follow your heart to answer the question: "After I die, what happens to the energetic conditions I have created in this life?" The energetic ripples that you are creating in the great lake of uni-time do not stop upon death for death is no barrier to the energetic forms you have conditioned in your future. Time and space is no barrier to energy. The universe is a perfect organism to condition effects here and now at exactly the right moment for you to experience them when you need them. You too are an effect of your own causes and it is by this process of conditioning, across a boundless time and within an environment of infinite energy and potential, that you project the conditions for your rebirth into physical life.

The question is how and ***why*** does this happen?

Look at it like this; you ***believe*** you exist, don't you? Throughout this work I have stressed that what you believe to be true in your mind becomes true in your physical reality. Your i-go is the mental manifestation of your belief in 'me' so, if i-go believes that you are a fixed asset of a physical reality, the universe quite happily organizes around this mental creation with a physical reflection in your future. As you go through life attaching to events as 'me' and 'mine', you create energetic ripples for which you are responsible. Like the rambler throwing rubbish along the footpath, next time you come back, the rubbish will still litter your journey until you dispose of it properly.

Your attachments in life are like little energetic babies projected from the mental form into the physical, from potentiality into actuality, from the present into a future present, simply awaiting the arrival of your consciousness to become actualized. Until you learn how to disconnect from i-go, disconnect from events as they happen, disconnect from the reaction as it happens, disconnect from the projection and disconnect from the recreation, you will continue to create energetic obligations for which you are held physically responsible in your future.

In boundless time, unaffected by physical death, the energy that you have projected into your future is the condition to ensure your physical birth in the next life. Energy respects none of the barriers we perceive in our physical world. The ripples are a natural karmic mechanism reflecting back at you everything you believe to be 'I', 'me' and 'mine', as these are the causal conditions for you to exist in the physical form for as long as you continue to condition yourself to exist.

Maintaining i-go is akin to attaching to energy that is not

yours to keep. It is also the ultimate illusion of 'mine'. I-go conditions your physical return so your energetic debt can be repaid. As soon as you have detached from all your emotional, physical, mental and spiritual attachments, the physical world will reflect no further conditions in which you exist. At that point, you will not exist. I-go will have died. The irony is that 'you' never really existed, other than as a set of conditions that you believed to be real.

Why Good Things Happen to Bad People

The one life theory confounds our comprehension of why seemingly random events happen in life and causes great emotional confusion and suffering. Perceived through the goggles of i-go, powerful events in life never fail to arouse frustration and bitterness. Seemingly random bouts of luck or misfortune leave us cursing events we don't seem to deserve or resentful of those who are blessed with events that they don't seem to have earned. Sometimes, these arbitrary events may cause people to blame God or provoke outrage at the apparent ambivalence of a universe without conscience or care.

In healing sessions, many of my clients have had traumatic lives and part of assimilating this trauma into spiritual growth begins by simply placing it in a different context than that of being a victim. It is like the rock falling from the sky: is it a victim of gravity? If we blame natural laws for working as they should we end up in a war with the entire physical and spiritual structure of the environment we have been born into. To create peace we must live in harmony with those laws and start to accept that our lives are not a product of a vengeful God, bad/good luck or other people's mistakes. ***You*** are the creator and your own life is your ultimate creation.

Remember chaos? All chaos really represents is the inability of the human mind to link an effect with a cause. Yet we can assume that no event is causeless and something cannot arise from nothing. When these seemingly chaotic events occur, they are actually the beautiful, effortless, elegant evidence of universal karma conditioning effects from your past lives to arise in your present reality. Their fruition in the present moment, however powerful and desperate they may feel, offers you the opportunity to generate a deeper understanding of the 'me' that created them and the underlying mind rafts supporting their rebirth in your present.

Only by substituting the mind raft of a separate and disconnected i-go with one that transcends multiple lives can this life's bewildering dramas become intelligible, valuable and be lived with genuine gratitude. It is a far simpler and more elegant proposition to live in a universe where you are ultimately accountable for yourself, your personal development and your choices than it is to live in one where accidents happen, miracles occur and fortunes are random. Remember, these are mind rafts, not absolute truths. As you journey forth through life, ask yourself whether the mind raft of a single life or multiple lives causes you less pain and suffering and then choose accordingly.

When we reject the idea of multiple lives we also relinquish the responsibility of spiritual purpose for which every being is accountable. I believe that every human being is actually aware of their spiritual purpose but not necessarily in their brain. Your physical body, your energetic body, your spirit, each is entwined and dependent upon one another. Each 'knows' what the other knows. You are here not only to experience living and dying physically but to use the physical world to transcend the obvious and 'kill yourself' through a kind of i-go 'suicide', if you will. This may sound a little melodramatic but it is intended to underscore the immense fear of death that emanates, I believe, not just from the prospect of rotting to physical dust but in the great spiritual fear that we have of letting go forever our attachments to the physical world of 'I', 'me' and 'mine'. This process may take many, many life times for most people, but in each life the challenges we face in the physical realm are actually urging us, cajoling us or even forcing us to face our spiritual integrity and become masters of our spiritual destiny.

Sadly, most people become so ensnared by the material world, the gross environment, that the subtle dimensions of life's spiritual objectives are hidden from them. The extreme result of this can be suicide, choosing to end physical existence because someone can perceive no physical means of ending the pain within them. It is a spiritual suffering that afflicts them and they are blind to it. Their spirit is literally aching for change but the i-go clings to the idea that 'I' am in pain, the suffering is 'mine' and ending 'me' will end the pain. It will not. Here on this physical earth, it is easy for spiritual purpose to achieve a physical surrogate but once this occurs and we reject the very notion of spirituality, despair can be the result. Once life becomes so entirely physical, the only death we can imagine is of the body. Our pain builds up in the physical and mental world and we close off our potential to release this pain through spiritual practice.

You exist to reduce yourself, your i-go, to a nothingness that ultimately connects to everything, not nothing. This task is both exhilarating, empowering and provides your existence the greatest meaning, but it is also a leap of faith that requires each of us to ponder and consider the prospect of total self-annihilation, the ultimate fear. I-go chooses surrogate purposes in life in order to sustain the illusory notion of self and consequently avoid the fearful prospect of its own death. The mind, grounded only in i-go, understands the opposite of life to be death and the opposite of something to be nothing and so, beyond life, we see only the prospect of physical death and nothingness.

Only faith can destroy fear. This is why faith is the purest form of spiritual power, a point that is also not lost in religious appreciation of spirituality. It has been understood since time began that faith bridges the gap between life's experiential lessons and the fear that encourages us to avoid them. Faith says everything that happens is significant. There is not a passing sound, a fleeting touch, a momentary event, a single object, person, thought, word or action that is not accounted for and significant. The universe doesn't make mistakes. As we begin to demand personal awareness over ignorance and faith over fear, slowly the present moment becomes the nexus of all time and events passing before us and, if we remain detached and observant of them, their passing away and dying is consistent with our own.

Death is the ultimate purpose of all things as well as the giver of life to all things. Condition your i-go to fade, to become meaningless, to lose control, to be evicted from the infinite home of your mind and you do not fade, become meaningless, lose control or disappear. You gain a home. You create a space from which profound universal truth sweeps away suffering and fills that home with the realization that your life's greater spiritual purpose is at hand: unity.

Chapter 10

Human Spirit

"We allow our ignorance to prevail upon us and make us think we can survive alone, alone in patches, alone in groups, alone in races, even alone in genders."

Maya Angelou - American poet, Memoirist, Actress, Civil Rights Leader and Author (1928-)

The 20 Attributes of Human Spirit

In Buddhism there is a metaphor called Indra's net. It describes a cavernous room filled with crystals, each suspended from the high ceiling at a different length. When a single beam of light is shone into the room, the entire room is illuminated as the light passes through each crystal and illuminates the next. Imagine one of these crystals to be you and you will see that the light illuminating you is no different from that which illuminates everyone else. You are not separate, you are connected. You are not independent, you are interdependent. Each soul or spirit is needed to illuminate the next. A single shared beam of light illuminates us all.

Unity is the natural state of all parts and pieces in the universe, so why do we not feel connected with other people? Why is it that society seems to be fragmenting, neighborhoods seem to be falling apart, even the foundation of family seems to be crumbling in many countries? If every spirit is connected to the next and each is needed to illuminate the next, why is it so hard to *feel* this connection? What is it about the current state of humanity that compels us to force each other away instead of bringing us together as one?

It is without doubt that i-go is the culprit. We have become so comfortable with its presence that we do not even suspect it of causing the damage that we do to ourselves and to our relationships with one another. We have already spent enough pages unveiling the villain, now we must target relational solutions through which anyone on this planet can find a connection with another human being and no longer claim ignorance of where to look.

I first discovered the concept of 'Human Spirit' in Bill Gould's Transformational Thinking program, which I taught alongside him for a number of years. At that time, as is true today, there were hundreds of systems claiming to define who you are and what you are made of but none of them seemed totally positive and each accused you of being in some way incomplete. The human spirit, according to Transformational Thinking, is 20 different attributes that comprise the complete human being. We all possess all 20 of these attributes but we each have predominant attributes that arise most frequently and account for our unique personal habits and characteristics.

The beauty of the 20 attributes of the human spirit is that every one of them is positive. There are no negative attributes and its crowning glory is how it achieves this positivity. Each of the 20 attributes represents an intrinsic human trait but each also has a corresponding need. Should we approach a person by fulfilling this need we will achieve a positive relational response because our approach is spirit-based. But, should we approach the person through i-go and violate their needs, a negative result is guaranteed.

Here is a breakdown of the 20 attributes and their corresponding needs, kindly printed with the permission of Dr. Bill Gould. As you go through them, make a metal note of those attributes that best represent who you think you are and how important the corresponding need is for your sense of wellbeing:

1. **Self-conscious Being (Needs Recognition)**
   The self-conscious Being is aware of itself. It communes with itself. There is always self-talk taking place. This attribute accounts for our self-awareness and self-contemplation. It leads us in our quest for self-fulfillment. It permits us to form images of ourselves, reflect upon our internal nature and esteem ourselves. This is the attribute that knows, intuitively, that "I exist and have meaning and significance".

2. **Self-determined Being (Needs Involvement)**
   The Self-Determined being is volitional, possessing the power and freedom to choose. It is very conscious of the act of choice and cherishes it. It is self-governing and autonomous and resents outside interference with individual liberty and freedom. Within this attribute lies free will.

3. **Propositional Being (Needs Logic)**
   The Propositional Being attribute is predominantly represented by the left-side of the brain. It deals in logic and reason, concepts and principles. At the same time, it deals very well with generalizations, classifications, and inference. It loves knowledge and thrives on analytical thinking. It is the seat of synthesis, wisdom, evaluation, memory, comprehension and interpretation. We rely on it for quantifying, measuring, and accuracy.

4. **Intelligent Being (Needs Explanation)**
   The attribute of the Intelligent Being is responsible for our fascination with and love of language theory, conceptual thinking ability, all spelling, reading, and writing. It constantly seeks symbols and responds to metaphorical examples. It drives us to preserve our history and information, always seeking to link us in time to the past and the future. It also loves semantics, naming, defining, labeling,

explaining, and all forms of communication. It deals in representational systems and has an immense propensity for mathematics and numbers. It is always seeking knowledge, desires exactness and strives for continual learning.

5. **Emotional Being (Needs Support)**
The Emotional Being is affective, showing all emotions and feelings. It reflects anger, passion, hate, love, humor, happiness, excitement, loneliness, sadness, gratitude and fear. It is very closely allied with the Creative and Social attributes.

6. **Social Being (Needs Inclusion)**
This is the relational attribute. The Social Being needs bonding, companionship, and love. It is communicative and trusting in nature. It is that part of us that reaches out to others and gives, as well as receives. It is the basis of appreciation and gratitude.

7. **Physical Being (Needs Space)**
The Physical Being attribute is the bonding of body/mind/spirit. It provides our sense of personal space and also provides the responses to our five senses of touch, smell, sight, sound and taste. It is the kinesthetic part of us in which we find our motor skills. It is that part of us that provides a sense of being in place.

8. **Purpose Being (Needs Reason)**
The Purpose attribute of our Being is one of the earliest awakenings of awareness. One of the first questions we ask (and never stop asking) is, "WHY?" The Purpose Being attribute establishes causes and supports them freely. It establishes relevance and identity. It needs to know that what we are and needs to feel that what we do has significance and meaning.

9. **Plan Being (Needs Direction)**

The Plan Being attribute is that part of us that projects into the future, providing a vital link between where we are and where we want to be. It is future and time oriented. It is also aware of the past and provides the internal link in space and time. It is goal and purpose driven, organizational and strategic. It loves to design and manage. It is methodical and calculating. It relishes technique and implementation. It is the actualizing attribute of the person.

10. **Principle Being (Needs Honesty)**

The Principle Being attribute provides our intuitive sense of right and wrong. It is the "belly barometer". It feels guilt and shame, feels responsible and accountable. It is the basis for character and moral conscience. It is the law maker and creed maker. It provides our internal code of ethics and moral values.

11. **Visionary Being (Needs Challenge)**

Where would we be without the Visionary Being attribute? It is this attribute that provides our dreams and fantasies. It is the designer within us, the tool maker, the design and tool user. It establishes high expectations and seeks to meet them. It is the seat of our ambition and responsiveness to challenge. It is the goal setter and adventurer.

12. **Worship Being (Needs Faith)**

It is the Worship Being that provides us with our propensity to worship and gives us a sense of a higher power and purpose. It is our God-consciousness, providing for the establishment of 360 faiths and 11 major religions. It is the basis for our need for mythology and mystery. It is founded in a deep inner faith. It thrives on grace, forgiveness, love, and patience.

13. Harmonious Being (Needs Balance)

The Harmonious Being attribute provides us with the need for balance and harmony, being one of the strongest driving natural attributes we possess. It likes structure, alignment, congruence, and accord. It needs moderation, and established boundaries and symmetry in all things.

14. Security Being (Needs Safety)

The Security Being attribute is one of the most basic of all human attributes. It requires safety and freedom from threat or danger. It is the basis for survival. It is the "fight or flight" attribute, needing basics such as sustenance and shelter. This attribute is also the basis for our adaptability and response to change, both external and internal.

15. Aesthetic Being (Needs Order)

The Aesthetic Being is that part of us which is perceptive and appreciates beauty and grace, elegance, and refinement. It likes culture, proportion, balance, form, orderliness, and cleanliness. The Aesthetic Being has strong moral sensibility. But it also possesses that sense of awe, that spirit of adventure one experiences when watching a sunset.

16. Trust Being (Needs Openness)

The Trust Being attribute is that part of us which harbors belief, values, faith, confidence, dependability, authenticity, commitment, and reliability. We want and need to trust and be trusted. It sets high expectations and is the basis for all meaningful relationships, along with respect.

17. Love Being (Needs Respect)

The Love Being is that part of us that requires companionship, relationships, personal commitments, affection, devotion, passion, tenderness, and bonding. It needs to know that there is value and worth in a relationship. It demands consideration and nurturing. It is that part of us that continually seeks to give more than it receives. It is the primary driving force for many people.

18. Leisure Being (Needs Time)

This is probably the one attribute we all wish we had more of. The Leisure Being likes ease and calm, prefers to be undisturbed, and likes to be entertained and amused. It is fun loving and relishes games. It is very much in tune to the creative attribute. It also strives for convenience and simplicity.

19. Intuitive Being (Needs Trust)

This is the part of us that loves to play with ideas, concepts, plans, and designs. It is predominantly a right-brained attribute, which follows hunches, trusts gut feelings and goes far beyond logic and reason. It is the seat of our imagination and the part of us that loves lateral thinking. It allows us to visualize and project. It is the source of all ideation and perception.

20. Creative Being (Needs Freedom)

The Creative Being is the inventor, the artist, the poet, the musician, the discoverer, and adventurer. It is this attribute that provides us with imagination, reason, ambiguity, and metaphor. It loves problem solving, theorizing, hypothesizing, laterally thinking, and ideation. It is inquisitive and questioning. It is horizon-expanding. It loves to marvel and wonder, and has a fascination for the unknown, always seeking new challenges.

Although each of these attributes has very unique characteristics, you will find connections and interconnections between them all.

They were designed to compliment and dovetail with one another and are not intended to demarcate independent pieces of a person. Organic permeable boundaries exist between one and the next as they exist between all things. This gives the model a feel closer to the great nuances distinguishing one person from another and one character trait from the next. Certain connections are obvious, such as between the intelligent and propositional beings, both characteristics of the mind, or the creative and leisure beings, requiring freedom and time but connections exist between them all if you care to look deeply enough.

As you examine the entire list of 20 attributes, you will probably notice three or four that stand out as the best representation of who you think you are. These will be your predominant attributes. Although you may spend much of your time in one of these modes, this does not mean that the others are not present within you too. Your character may merely be less inclined to exhibit their traits. As you go through your day, different tasks and events will trigger different attributes to arise and thus your needs change too. If you go into a work meeting, you may be in Purpose Being mode, needing reason or Plan Being needing direction. At home you may be in Leisure Being needing time or Social Being needing inclusion in activities with your family. Each situation brings about a different being from within you and each being has different requirements and expectations. Clearly, if people meet your needs because they are sensitive, aware and responsive to your state of mind, the resulting outcome in both relational and physical terms is likely to be an improvement on what they would get if they related to you without awareness, sensitivity or with purely selfish objectives.

The great power of the human spirit model is that these attributes are not difficult to identify in other people. Go back through the list and find a different friend or associate who is a good example of predominance in each attribute. It doesn't matter whether this person is your life partner with whom you interact every day or an acquaintance who you have met only once five years ago. When you approach anyone with the genuine intention to fulfill the needs of their human spirit you will receive a profound reaction from them whether you have correctly identified their predominant need or not. Who doesn't need respect, space, order, involvement or reason in their life? These are all basic human needs. How would your relationships improve if you met every one on the basis of fulfilling their needs? The world would clearly benefit from each of us ratcheting up the selflessness of spirit and toning down the selfishness of i-go whoever we are.

Returning to the model of yin-yang i-go that we looked at in a previous chapter, you will now see how the human spirit model works to bring balance to the entire model.

Human Spirit 'Being'	**Needs**	**Yin I-Go Excess**	**Harmonious Human Spirit**	**Yang I-Go Excess**
Self-Conscious	Recognition	Shy	Self-Confident	Arrogant
Self-Determined	Involvement	Indecisive	Decisive	Dictatorial
Propositional	Logic	Assumptive	Analytical	Argumentative
Intelligent	Explanation	Naive	Inquisitive	Critical
Emotional	Support	Repressed	Empathetic	Needy
Social	Inclusion	Reclusive	Bonds Well	Manipulative
Physical	Space	Sanctimonious	Sensitive	Hedonistic
Purpose	Reason	Unfocused	Determined	Fanatical
Plan	Direction	Fearful	Strategic	Controlling
Principle	Honesty	Amoral	Consistent	Hypocritical
Visionary	Challenge	Conforming	Challenge-Seeking	Fantasizing
Worship	Faith	Faithless	Spiritual	Zealous
Harmonious	Balance	Undiscerning	Impartial	Prejudiced
Security	Safety	Vulnerable	Confident	Arrogant
Aesthetic	Orderliness	Disorderedly	Graceful	Ostentatious
Trust	Openness	Secretive	Transparent	Gullible

Love	Respect	Alienating	Accepting	Doting
Leisure	Time	Easily Bored	Uses Free Time Creatively	Wastes Time
Intuitive	Trust	Skeptical	Faith	Whimsical
Creative	Freedom	Ineffective	Constructive	Impractical

The right three columns elucidate the internal yin and yang reactive mode that your i-go conditions dependent upon your personal characteristics. The middle column of the three, the harmonious spirit, offers you a guide towards greater personal integrity, honesty and transparency. On the other side of the chart, the human spirit and corresponding needs columns uses the same 20 attributes to expound an external approach to conditioning reality. With awareness of yourself, you calm i-go and with awareness of others, you maintain and develop relationships increasingly based upon spirit.

The human spirit model reinforces the timeless lesson that treating others as we would like to be treated ourselves is an energetic investment in spirit that conditions your entire relational environment in a very different way than i-go ever could. Meeting each person and giving them just what they need is an awesome approach to relationships that sets up an energetic condition that is simply impossible when we are focused upon 'me' and 'mine'. Just imagine what would happen both inside and outside if you were able to defuse your i-go defense for a few days, practice giving people what they need, however inconvenient and alien this may initially feel to your nature, while simultaneously seeking to bring the deficiencies and excess of the i-go into alignment with your spirit? Try it and see what happens.

Throughout Provolution you have learned that the external reality, conditioned by you, reflects and conditions the internal reality just as the internal reality reflects and conditions the external reality. It should now be apparent how your personal transformation is a process where both yin and yang, inside and outside, quiet introspection and deliberate action are needed to generate a harmony where i-go is stilled in all planes simultaneously so that none remains to infuse uni-time with the conditions for its rebirth. If you can do this with courage, without flinching, without fear, you will be tapping into an energy that is entirely the opposite of what created i-go in the first place. It is your authentic human spirit.

Chapter 11

U-go

"If we could raise one generation with unconditional love, there would be no Hitlers. We need to teach the next generation of children from Day One that they are responsible for their lives. Mankind's greatest gift, also its greatest curse, is that we have free choice. We can make our choices built from love or from fear."

Dr. Elizabeth Kubler-Ross – Swiss-born psychiatrist and Author (1926 – 2004)

The Relational Mirror

In this chapter we are going to look at relationships on a deeper level entirely. We are first going to learn about the relational mirror, how your perceptions of other people are actually a reflection of yourself. From this you will discover how to use your reactions to people as wonderful insights into your own i-go. Secondly, we will look at the ultimate relational responsibility: unconditional love and acceptance, which will lead us to question how responsible we really are for the relationships in our life. If we are truly interconnected and interdependent, can we really separate one person's suffering from our own and, if not, do we have to accept total responsibility for our part in creating the suffering that exists around us?

We have already established that your perception of the world is subjective and uniquely yours. Every experience that enters your mind through your senses is translated through the filter of your i-go, so when you meet another person, the same process occurs. This means that your perception of a person is not objective. You do not meet a fixed, permanent person. A person who is experienced by three different people will be perceived in three different ways, as if three people reside inside him/her. Although we may label a person kind, mean, happy, content or sad and achieve a certain accord among other people who know that person, everyone will actually perceive someone different. So, when you meet a person, who do you actually meet?

U-go is the answer. U-go is the reaction you have to another person's i-go based upon your own. How you react and feel about another person's behavior is really a reflection of yourself because you can only relate to other people through the filter of your current perception, which will essentially be i-go-based. Unless you have learned to meet people with a totally unconditioned mind, which is unlikely, your relationships routinely activate all the little switches conditioned into your own library of reactions so that you project your own self onto them and experience a little piece of you each time you meet them.

U-go acts like a ***relational mirror***. Everyone you meet is an opportunity to learn something new about yourself. If you react to a person angrily, where does the anger come from? Not from them. They may provide the trigger but the trigger for what? The anger was already inside you, conditioned and waiting to reveal itself. If you perceive your anger as someone else's fault, you miss the lesson entirely and simply get into your own i-go's shame and blame game. On the other hand, use u-go as a tool to recognize the types of behaviors you are attracting into your life and the reactions they trigger inside you and other people gradually become the external stimuli by which you generate greater sensitivity and awareness to the conditions you have been responsible for creating inside yourself.

Whether a cause for celebration or regret, at this point in Provolution, you now understand that your life is not a collection of random situations. Events arise because you have conditioned them to arise. This is no less true of people in your life. By accepting that energy transcends your physical existence and conditions life after life, then those people who enter your reality today are conditioned to be there too and you have spent many lifetimes sharing your experience of one another. You exist because you have conditioned your existence. Others exist because you have conditioned their existence. You exist because others have conditioned your existence. This is the awesome nature of an interconnected and interdependent universe. Are you getting used to it yet?

Every relationship in your life is a mutually conditioned energetic debt waiting to be settled. Sometimes people are here to inspire you to greatness, sometimes they are here to challenge and conflict with you. It is difficult to perceive others with the gratitude or compassion they deserve when you are unaware of their full significance. Other people accelerate your personal transformation through your experience of them and them through you. They place you in situations or inspire you to feel in ways that you could never experience without them and would often never choose with free will. Their energy, their presence, is a catalyst for your personal growth and practicing acceptance and gratitude for everyone in your life is a very powerful way of creating personal peace.

Learning to observe your u-go reactions to other people is exactly the same process as learning to observe your arising emotions in uni-time and detaching from them. You can do nothing truly creative and meaningful in your life outside the present moment so, if you extend your meditative practice to stay centered in the present throughout your day, you will catch yourself reacting within the old i-go template. Observe this without judgment and you can begin to release the inherent energy and reset the old reactive patterns. Being sensitive to your initial response to a person and aware that it is a product of your i-go thus allows you to connect with other people's human spirit. Approach that person as an opportunity for you to fulfill their spiritual needs and incredible things begin to happen. Your own human spirit begins to shine through too. Since other people are a reflection of you, would you expect any different?

In this awareness, your relational objective becomes, not winning, not taking, not controlling, but parting without energetic debt. When you remove i-go from your relationships and begin to view others as an honest reflection of yourself, a deeper compassion arises in you for you know that each person who enters your life has endured suffering relative to your own and are stuck, just as you are, in cycles that condition them to repeat feelings and energies that they cannot release without your mutual participation. When you meet people seeking to end their suffering, this is the first step to relationships built entirely from love.

Unconditional Love

There is a powerful shaman from Hawaii called Dr. Ihaleakala Hew Len who has an amazing story to tell. He learned a Hawaiian technique called ho'oponopono, which means, "to make right", or "to rectify an error". The traditional ho'oponopono philosophy stems from an ancient teaching originally called Ho'omana. 'Ho'o' means to make. 'Mana' means life force, which is equivalent to qi that we looked at earlier. Thus, Ho'omana actually means to empower, which is an apt description of what the philosophy is all about in application. Ho'omana is believed by its practitioners to be around 35,000 years old and its modern application is taught today under the name 'Huna'. Dr. Len has spent many years working with such organizations as UNESCO, International Human Unity Conference on World Peace and Healers for Peace in Europe teaching the tenets of this incredible practice of self-love and forgiveness. The belief system of ho'oponopono is very simple but it turns the traditional perception of responsibility on its head and offers you the power to quite literally transform your suffering into wellness for everyone you meet.

Ho'oponopono teaches that you are ***entirely responsible*** for

everyone and ***everything*** that happens in your life. Reread that sentence if you are as surprised and skeptical as I was when I first heard about it some years ago. Yes, you are ***completely responsible*** for everything that happens, not just those events where you are identifiably the cause, nor just those people who you have a direct impact upon, but everything and everyone whether in a distant part of the globe or right here on your doorstep. We have already learned how chaos separates us physically from events but connects us through the intangible energetic interconnectivity and interdependence of nature. Ho'oponopono is a practical application of this belief centered around some ridiculously simply practices that only begin to make sense when you have abandoned the mind raft of separation and grasped the interdependence that renders all u-go's a creation of yourself. Dr. Len tells an incredible story of how he applied ho'oponopono to an entire ward of psychiatric patients in Hawaii, resulting in a transformation that, according to conventional wisdom, is impossible and yet it is not a myth. It really happened and it is described in the book "Zero Limits", co-written by Dr. Len and Joe Vitale. I include here some portions of this amazing story:

> *(Dr. Len) explained that he worked at Hawaii State Hospital for four years. That ward where they kept the criminally insane was dangerous. Psychologists quit on a monthly basis. The staff called in sick a lot or simply quit. People would walk through that ward with their backs against the wall, afraid of being attacked by patients. It was not a pleasant place to live, work, or visit.*
>
> *Dr. Len told me that he never saw patients. He agreed to have an office and to review their files. While he looked at those files, he would work on himself. As he worked on himself, patients began to heal.*
>
> *"After a few months, patients that had to be shackled were being allowed to walk freely," he told me. "Others who had to be heavily medicated were getting off their medications. And those who had no*

chance of ever being released were being freed." I was in awe. "Not only that," he went on, "but the staff began to enjoy coming to work.

Absenteeism and turnover disappeared. We ended up with more staff than we needed because patients were being released, and all the staff was showing up to work. Today, that ward is closed."

This is where I had to ask the million dollar question: "What were you doing within yourself that caused those people to change?"

"I was simply healing the part of me that created them," he said. I didn't understand. Dr. Len explained that total responsibility for your life means that everything in your life, simply because it is in your life, is your responsibility. In a literal sense the entire world is your creation.

Zero Limits – The Secret Hawaiian System for Wealth, Health, Peace, and More, Joe Vitale & Dr. Ihaleakala Hew Len, Wiley (June 2007)

I'm sure you will want to read that again and digest its fullest implications before we move on. What Dr. Len was explaining to Vitale was interconnection and interdependence taken to an unconditional level, that of unconditional love through acceptance of everyone's inherent connection with you. When you take interconnection and interdependence beyond the mental comprehension that you are connected to me and us to them and we to it there comes a point when you begin to suspect that interdependence has an even deeper implication that evades most of us totally because its implications blow away conventional thinking and logic. Here's what Dr. Len says about it:

"If you take complete responsibility for your life, then everything you see, hear, taste, touch, or in any way experience is your responsibility because it is in your life. This means that terrorist activity, the president, the economy or anything you experience and don't

like – is up for you to heal. They don't exist, in a manner of speaking, except as projections from inside you. The problem isn't with them, it's with you, and to change them, you have to change you."

I asked Dr. Len how he went about healing himself. What was he doing, exactly, when he looked at those patients' files? "I just kept saying, 'I'm sorry' and 'I love you' over and over again." "That's it?" I said. "That's it."

Zero Limits – The Secret Hawaiian System for Wealth, Health, Peace, and More, Joe Vitale & Dr. Ihaleakala Hew Len, Wiley (June 2007)

We do not understand unconditional love nor do we practice it in any of our relationships. Dr. Len's application of ho'oponopono is unconditional love that began by loving and accepting himself and the creations for which he is responsible in his reality. In a legal or social sense, if we accept responsibility for creating someone else's suffering we assume guilt and are thus worthy of punishment. However, we must escape this damning cycle of thought if we are to fully accept responsibility for reality and change it without fear and regret that things are the way they are. Dr. Len accepted responsibility for those in his reality but he did so with unconditional love for himself, without shame, without blame. Only then was he capable of extending that love outside to everyone whom he had accepted responsibility for conditioning. In this way he began to undo the suffering inside himself and its reflective counterpart on the outside. This is the relational mirror taken to a whole different level and it is a level through which me, you and our entire global society can provolve and escape the cycle of suffering that we have created together.

Few of us can attest to loving ourselves unconditionally, for we do not believe, deep down in our hearts, that we deserve it. Why? Because we have not been taught to give unconditionally. There must always be a reason for the reward, a completed goal or something exceptional before praise is earned. We forget that we are already exceptional. We are already perfect. We are born into a human body and are here, now. That should be enough but it isn't because we do not live in a paradigm of spiritual acceptance, but a paradigm of i-go judgment.

As children, many of us were conditioned to believe we were bad, naughty, selfish, indeed, we may even have been deliberately bad or naughty to rebel or spite those we felt were controlling us. Ho'oponopono teaches that the internal suffering is reflected in the external projection and thus, those people who bless your life with their presence are suffering outside of you in just the same way as you suffer inside. You have contributed to their pain just by being who you are but this does not mean you are bad or undeserving of your own deepest love and respect. Quite the contrary, in fact. Love will heal you. You have affected the collective reality by spicing the uni-time soup with your unique energy. You do this simply be being you. It is a fine contribution. Accepting yourself for who you are begins with accepting that your challenge is your internal pain. It is not your punishment. It is a signpost; an opportunity to heal yourself and others.

Normal human relationships are virtually always conditional because we expect something in return for what we give out. If I love you, I expect you to love me too. Moreover, I expect love to be demonstrated according to my desires and not in ways I wish to avoid. If we can share conditional love on my terms (which may change as I develop through the years) then I can claim to love you and my love for you will endure but if you do not meet my expectations, I will become disappointed, my love may turn to anger or bitterness or jealousy and then we are in a different kind of relationship all together. Which of us loves without any conditions at all?

You may believe that unconditional love is impossible or impractical, then it becomes impossible and impractical to you but ho'oponopono says it is both practical, possible and a necessary step in human evolution to accept reality for what it is and not what it seems to be. Anyone, anywhere, regardless of status, age, wealth or any of the other factors we routinely list as excuses for maintaining the status quo can claim to be unable to say "I love you. Please forgive me". Yet how many of us will dismiss such a seemingly powerless practice because it is beyond the current capacity of our mind to imagine what our heart is currently unable to feel? Without doubt practicing the tenets of ho'oponopono requires a commitment to change what we currently believe to be our degree of responsibility for the reality we have created, but what are the potential benefits of doing so? In short: liberation from your suffering by accepting the interconnection and interdependence of everyone who enters your reality.

Our u-go projections of other people reveal the state of turmoil that exists within us. The i-go cannot comprehend why we should unconditionally love anyone we judge unworthy of it and this includes ourselves. Yet we only need survey a world of appalling injustice, great conflict, disrespect and distrust spiraling around us to experience the alternative. I-go always divides, separates and creates conflict whereas the spirit of unconditionality joins, connects and forges unity. The very word 'unconditional' defines the nature of true love, for it is so pure that it arises without force, expects nothing in return and creates no karma around it. It neither conditions nor needs conditioning. Once we accept people for who and what they are, not what we wish them to be or wish they weren't, love will arise quite naturally.

A world where each of us recognizes and accepts our responsibility for the suffering that exists in us and around us is not so far off. Provolution is not only possible, it is happening. More and more ancient teachings like ho'oponopono are being revealed and applied by people who are discarding mind rafts that no longer serve their purpose and accepting that the universe is not only the bricks and mortar environment that their left brain has defined as real. It is subtle. It is adaptable. It ultimately creates what you ***believe*** to be real and what you have created is a result of what you have believed.

Moreover, as ho'oponopono elegantly demonstrates, it is hardly rocket science to spend a couple of moments with each person you meet asking what you need to heal inside yourself to heal them. It is hardly a chore to whisper inside of you "I love you, I am sorry, please forgive me" or, as the human spirit suggests, ask what it is they need from you to be happy. This is the choice to provolve the way you perceive your place in the world around you and accept each person you have been blessed with. Whatever position in society you attain, whatever income you earn, whatever house you own, the greatest thing you will ever create in this life is you. This is the spirit of unconditional acceptance for who you are and the root of being ready to unconditionally offer this acceptance to others around you. Such behavior engenders an environment of abundance where everyone is giving and there is more than enough to go around.

Chapter 12

We-go

"The most important principle of divine philosophy is the oneness of the world of humanity, the unity of mankind, the bond conjoining East and West, the tie of love which blends human hearts."
Abdu'l-Bahá - Head of the Bahá'í Faith (1844 – 1921)

Changing the World One Person at a Time

Chaos invites us all to contribute ourselves to a shared reality. The monk in Tibet contributes, the street vendor in Caracas contributes, the Mafioso in New York contributes, the business owner in Riyadh contributes; the weak, the strong, the happy and the sad all contribute to the reality that is collective, shared and our mutual responsibility. If you want to provolve that reality, it is up to you to adjust your contribution to the chaos and begin contributing in the same way you would wish others to contribute towards your own freedom and peace. Perhaps then, they would.

Fueling a provolution in human spirit requires a fundamental expansion of consciousness within ordinary people. It takes a long walk in the shoes of the many disenfranchised to understand that we are failing to meet their human spirit needs and thus failing the responsibilities of interconnected and interdependent relationships. We do not know these people. We never will. But, if we are ever to know ourselves, our true personal potential, we must find good reasons to care for those billions mired in the blindness of i-go or tethered to conditions that condemn them to physical drudgery. Our species' very intention must evolve from selfish independence to selfless cooperation and our vision become no less utopian than building societies where all people on earth have the opportunity to explore their true self. It is ***we-topia*** we should seek: a state of consciousness that balances the emotional, physical, spiritual and mental needs of 'me' and 'us', and fulfills them both by removing the conditioning that binds people to the i-go's spiral of suffering. If we understand the absolute necessity of attaining a symbiotic relationship between the needs of the i-go and the needs of the we-go, contentment in both becomes possible and social wounds can be healed.

Our current social models fail to work because they sacrifice the prospects of either 'me' or 'us' in favor of one or the other. I firmly believe that this is an unnecessary compromise born only from i-go fears. Any political or social ideology that subverts either is fatally flawed. Communism failed because it could not serve the diverse and idiosyncratic needs of real people and our innate desire for self-expression. But capitalism is also failing because it compels people to be competitive and prioritize their individual need for survival above others. Both are unsustainable. A society built upon control and homogenized, submissive people is no less damaging to the human spirit than one built upon competition and selfish-individualism. We can do better.

Many people will claim that we-topia is impossible. If we each deny our role in creating it and are immune from the potential within us to do so, this is undoubtedly true. Yet I have faith that people will begin provolving the global conditions by shining a light in their particular corner of reality where no one else can do the work. Provolution begins through the enormous challenge of self-improvement, which, surprisingly, is a far greater challenge than global transformation. While we deny the potential for global change, we also deny our personal duty to overcome the limits of our i-go and expand the we-go connections that facilitate a we-topian environment.

The i-go is great at justifying the status quo. Indeed, it is the stunning centerpiece of it. We spend endless mental resources convincing ourselves that our part in the enduring reality is inevitable because provolution is 'impractical' or 'naïve' but such claims are the timeless sanctuary of those people who believe their personal limitations to be the yardstick of what is possible and what is not. We should no longer be so arrogant as to believe this true. It is a platitude indeed but whether you believe you can or believe you can't: ***you're right***. The world changes one person at a time and it starts with your personal attitude towards what is possible. ***Everything*** is possible. Everyday you create a life for yourself that is unique, stunning and, if you consider the infinite machinations and interdependencies that create it, virtually impossible but still you manage to do it whether you are trying to or not. Just imagine what becomes possible if provolution is your intention and you set up your entire world to make it happen? This life is all about doing what other people haven't done, thinking what hasn't been thought, speaking words that have never been spoken so that your unique personality, talents and abilities bless all of us with their inimitable individuality. It is your turn to explore just how unique you really are and create a life that is a showpiece of what seems impossible to many people. While they may perceive the grand purpose of society to be a job and a pay packet, we must transform this view into the intention to create a comprehensive social environment whose higher purpose is the opportunity for people to evolve: evolution of mind, evolution of learning, evolution of emotions, evolution of values, evolution of spirit, ***provolution;*** a positive transformation where each of us chooses what is possible and what is not.

You are part of the collective we-go, the tribal self of humanity. Through your thoughts, words and actions your energetic presence contributes your uniqueness to the interconnected universe. How do you wish to contribute? As a net giver or a net taker? As an optimistic motivator or a pessimistic cynic? As a barrier or a facilitator? Every time you think, speak and act you recreate your energetic presence, and to recreate it in a positive, vibrant, provolutionary form contributes to the entire human we-go comprised of millions of different nations, towns, companies, neighborhoods, communities and families. To change the world, you have to believe it is possible. While so many people contribute their energy to the mind rafts of what cannot be done, what can be done fades to the mundane. To be the light that never dies, all you need do is provolve a little closer to home.

Provolution Begins at Home

There is good reason why it is said that charity begins at home. Changing the world begins with your personal practice: awareness and sensitivity to your own i-go. You cannot get much closer to home than this. However, once you have begun to master your own i-go, your practice needs then extend outwards to those emotionally closest to you, specifically the we-go of family, the unique characteristics that exist in every family and define its personality and shape. You cannot expect peace in the Middle East (or anywhere else in the world for that matter) if you are at war in your own home.

I cannot recall a person who has had a therapy or healing session with my wife and I who has not had unresolved issues with their mother, father, sibling, spouse or child. Collectively, these familial relationships comprise your individual identity as well as contribute to the collective we-go in whose image you have fashioned your personal truth. Often I will talk to a client about their issue with a parent, for example, and they will deny that they have an issue. They are unaware of it because they have buried it deeply behind a wall of denial that allows them to ignore the pain of the situation and justify the i-go's automated response. They may say, "I don't even think about my mother," or "I am completely ambivalent about that person," but this is always a diversion from the underlying issues that lie at the core of a person's present moment and therefore impact upon the future they are creating.

We ***all*** have issues at home. Once we have begun to arrange the fractured pieces of our own mind, we can begin to see how these cracks connect us unerringly to the people closest to us in our lives. There are no accidents, no mistakes, no spooky reasons why the cracks have appeared in the first place. They are there to be healed and you can do that if you acknowledge their existence and assume responsibility for feeling better than you do about them.

How do you do create a 'me' that accepts your family whatever they have done and whatever they mean to you? You act in faith that your suffering creates theirs and work to heal yourself. You live in gratitude that your relatives are around to inspire you to be free from the feelings they invoke within you and that their right to express themselves in their unique way unfetters your own potential to feel and observe your reactions to them. You work to accept them as a reflection of your own suffering and by meeting the needs of their human spirit fulfill your own transition from a reactive i-go to an observing spirit. You don't have to make people love you. You don't have to be best friends with everyone. You just have to love yourself and stop hurting. That alone changes everything.

Whichever family member you are in conflict with, ***you*** can heal that relationship. They are not reading this book, ***you are*** and chaos tells you that change is possible if ***you*** change. Interdependence shows you why it works. Ho'oponopono shows how to create it. All that is missing is the right effort. You can be whoever you want to be and the quality of your relationships with others relies on who you become and what you heal within yourself. Your task is not to preach the merits of awareness to others but to demonstrate them by being different than you were yesterday, to keep practicing and keep growing as a spiritual being. Generate the conditions where peace can bloom in your life by being sensitive and aware of what it means to all your collective we-go's if you don't. Doing nothing ensures that your family environment reconditions the current reality and if you remain at war within yourself and those closest to you, the world remains a battlefield.

Contributing to a loving, compassionate, gentle family life is a powerful contribution to a loving, compassionate, gentle neighborhood, region, country and world. Chaos ensures that your every act of sensitivity is reflected back at you multidimensionally, in all levels of society and in all your relationships. However distant you think someone is from you, in quantum physics, everyone is your neighbor.

This does not mean you have to become submissive or appeasing. There is great power in finding yourself and setting boundaries of what is acceptable in your life and what is not. At the same time, nurturing forgiveness in your heart for any boundaries that have been crossed sows seeds of healing for everyone. When you are angry at others, this is not a signal for seeking revenge. Don't let other people control you by harboring emotions that justify your anger, resentment, bitterness, grief and guilt. Forgive yourself for the anger that resides within and you will find the strength to forgive them. Move on with your life and the world moves on with you. Let go of what you no longer need on the journey and continue unburdened. Each morning when you wake up, generate gratitude for being alive and for everyone who is with you on this journey of life. Their contribution makes you better than you ever could be alone. Each night before you go to bed, release every emotional attachment you may have carried through the day and forgive those who acted without sensitivity towards you. Accept that you are the creator of your reality and you gain the power to make it what you will.

The we-go of your family will not change overnight but it will change if you change. If you get better results in your life by respecting others around you, meeting the needs of their human spirit and practicing leaving your i-go outside the door each time you return home, you will quickly learn how to be sensitive and aware of your emotions arising and let them go rather than cling to them as I, me or mine. If you change, other people will see different parts of themselves in your relational mirror and respond differently. The u-go that you represent to them will shift and thus your relationship will gradually shift too. Find peace in your family environment and no peace will be a stranger to you.

But what of your workplace? Extend this sensitivity and awareness out to your occupational environment and you will experience a change in we-go there too. Those co-workers who you don't see eye to eye with, the boss who controls you, the subordinates who never listen: approach them afresh by fulfilling the needs of their human spirit and things *will* change. Better still, teach them all about the human spirit as a pledge to meet their needs and watch the transformation begin. Accept responsibility for why they are here and their role in your life miraculously transforms from burden to boon. All it took was a shift in perception. Don't worry about what you get back from others. Just be consistent with your application of your learning and people will eventually see that you are genuinely trying to connect to them, respect them, meet their needs and build bridges of trust, not conflict. If they do not wish to see this, they will probably leave, looking for a fight elsewhere, and you will be free from them anyway. Don't present a target and no one can strike you however many times they may hit out.

An even better strategy is to find work that suits the person you have become through provolution. Start your own company or find a company that is in better alignment with the new you and your spiritual purposes. Strangely enough, when you embark on provolution, connections to suitable jobs and opportunities will naturally open up. Creating the space in your life for evolution allows new opportunities to appear for you to evolve into. Let the universe worry how. That's what it does. You just have to believe the potential exists and is awaiting fruition. Risk only exists in the mind that perceives it and your job in life is not to struggle against risk but to open your eyes to opportunity. Be here and now and await the opportunity to present itself, clear in the awareness that you will have the courage to grab it when it appears.

Find groups that support who you want to be and live in ways that you want to live. In Buddhism they say that when the tiger comes down from the mountain, the villagers will kill it. This means that provolution on a mountaintop, away from society, is relatively easy because no one is present to destroy your high ambitions or critique your eccentric new habits. As you transform mind rafts and live by different values, you will become less and less familiar to others who wish to remain the same old 'me'. Expanding consciousness looks very different to static consciousness. Some may be motivated by it and wonder how you suddenly became so happy and bright. These people may follow in the path you have blazed. Others will be angry and intimidated that you have evolved beyond their comprehension but this is their choice, not yours. Just keep healing yourself and other people around you will heal, become attracted towards your healing and in turn heal others around them. In this way they pay energetic homage to your influence in the same way that the last domino affects the first.

In finding groups to meditate with, bond with and support each other, there will always be a shoulder to lean on, a hand to guide, a wise word during those tough times that are inevitable in a changing, chaotic universe. By creating a refuge, the tiger can come down from the mountain and be among friends. This is a fine lesson my wife and I have learned here on Phuket, Thailand, with our good friends Dorinda and Nikorn who hold weekly spiritual circles for sharing and discussion. There are plenty of people who have been where you are going and are happy to share with you where they've been. Do not be afraid to ask for help and seek out those who are waiting for you to arrive so that your suffering may heal theirs. Do not be afraid to be vulnerable. There is no strength in denial or pride and it is a truly wonderful liberation to be so acceptant of change that your i-go presents no barrier to it.

Take the step of starting a local group of your own. You don't have to be a master to share what you are learning and what you know. Only i-go will claim that you do. You will learn what you need as you go along. In your neighborhood there will be dozens, if not hundreds of people who are aware of how important it is to seek change and relief from the spiritual suffering that ails them. Everyone can learn how to let go of emotional pain, to live in uni-time, to unburden themselves of old mind rafts, to heal themselves through awareness and sensitivity. Teach them. Share with them. You can use this book as a discussion tool and work through it together to apply it to your lives.

You do not need a college degree or educational certificate to come together and share the means of liberation from your suffering. Find a way to overcome it in solidarity. Everyone can contribute their experience, just enter the process with a willingness to learn and grow. Understand that your suffering is dependent upon the group's and their suffering dependent upon yours. Finding peace together heals everyone. Cure the collective we-go by taking responsibility for your share of that suffering and bring people together to transfer your knowledge, experience and perceptions that open people's minds to their innate potential. Community provolution extends out from your own family and rekindles the connection between other families whose future is intimately connected and dependent with your own.

The Spiritual Bottleneck

According to the WWF's 'Living Planet Report' for 2008:

- In 2003, people were using 25 per cent more resources than the world was able to sustain.
- We have lost 30 per cent of the total biodiversity of the planet since 1970 and in the tropics this figure increases to 51 per cent.
- If our demands on the planet continue to increase at the same rate, by the mid-2030's we would need the equivalent of two planets to maintain our lifestyles.

What was most worrying about this report when I first began reading it in 2006 was not just that the world could effectively be sucked dry of resources by 2030 unless we radically change our habits but the nonchalant way that the general public seemed to accept the headlines that made international news at the time. No panic. No uproar. No outcry. Nothing. Why not? How come hundreds of millions of people are not hammering upon the doors of their leaders demanding the sea change in mind rafts that might stave off our impending extinction? Where is the global insistence on transformation in economic and social policy to facilitate it? Do we blithely assume that human ingenuity will invent some technological marvel to remove $C0^2$ from the atmosphere or that some new bio-crop will grow trees faster than we are using them or that we can simply clone the thousands of species of animal and plant life that we have thus far annihilated and continue to annihilate each day? Even as our entire species' survival prospects are threatened, we still do not connect the desolate state of our global environment with the derelict state of humanity's collective spirit.

Just a few weeks after the 2006 Living Planet Report was issued, British entrepreneur Sir Richard Branson offered 25 million dollars to the first person to invent a machine to take CO^2 from the atmosphere! Perhaps it would be a far more credible solution to offer a reward to the inventor of a machine that removes the i-go from the human mind, for this is the real root of the problem. We tend towards perceiving every social conundrum as a technological challenge awaiting economists or scientists to smooth us past each 'rocky patch' in our species' evolution, assuming that, when they do, the business of buying and selling the planet can carry on as normal. But it is time we woke up. This is not an economic problem. This is not a technological problem. It is a ***spiritual*** problem. All other issues faced by humanity today are connected to the 'ground zero' of all personal and global problems: ***'I', 'me' and 'mine'***. At the end of the day the solution stems from a simple choice. Do you choose a self-gratifying, competitive i-go-based lifestyle or a spirit-based, cooperative ***we-topia*** where contentment is not bought from outside but expanded from within? The answer to this question determines the immediate future direction of our global culture and, I believe, answers the question of whether our species will survive the process or not.

A wonderful quote from Kurt Vonnegut's 'Slaughterhouse Five' is: *"...she was trying to construct a life that made sense from things she found in gift shops."* How many people on earth are aspiring to that today? While we continue choosing to save our planet by tweaking the systems by which we spend and make money, this is little different to asking the gun-toting thug to innovate a more peaceful path towards hegemony. We will not change the root causes of our problems globally, locally or personally by merely shifting the issues around like we might shift the lumps in a bumpy mattress. We need a new mattress, which means expanding personal awareness of the mind rafts causing this collective problem and replacing them with better ones.

The explosion of mechanical power resulting from the industrial revolution has amplified the impact of human activity on planet earth and the impact of i-go-based thinking on every living species. Modern technological prowess has accelerated this impact even further through satellite networks and broadband communications systems. We stand on the brink of a global catastrophe with i-go and spiritual ignorance as its prime protagonist. For some centuries now it has been urgent, and essential in the last few decades, that we awaken to a human purpose beyond the acquisition of physical stuff and appreciate the spiritual bottleneck we have created on planet earth.

Each person on this planet is a spiritual being. We are in the physical realm to expand and explore our spirituality through physical stimulus but the earth is a unique and highly addictive physical environment in which to achieve this. It is easy for your mind to become attached to the physical experience and loathed to release it. When i-go becomes attached to so many times, so many places, so many people and so many things, the illusion of physicality becomes reality and the reality of our spirit becomes an illusion of faith.

This i-go illusion has created a spiritual bottleneck that symbolizes the connection between human over population and the current global ecological crisis faced by all species on earth. It is a final example of how our spiritual condition mirrors our physical and it could well be our last chance to read the signs.

The thoughts, feelings, objects or people that you energetically attach to in this life must be released before you can be released from your earthly obligations to them and escape the physical cycle of rebirth. If life were a job, like a good employee you would be required to return all your work tools, your uniform and your paperclips before you went home, right? On earth your tool is your mind and your job is to experience the energetic currency of thoughts, words and actions and to quit with no debt. Before you can be released from your lives on earth you must detach from the energy you have squirreled away inside your mind, body and spirit and leave it behind where it belongs and you don't!

The i-go-fueled social and economic conditions have produced physical overcrowding and the related depletion of natural resources through the spiritual process of rebirth. As physical mind rafts perpetuate through expanding i-go we also ensure our physical rebirth and more and more spirits are sucked into a maelstrom of suffering, unable to transcend their attachments. We have poured countless lifetimes' energy into the creation of entire social environments where physical matters are prioritized above all others, selfishness is commonsense and problems that are out of sight really stay out of mind. The prevailing global personal truth has become such a finely honed spiritual trap that the subtle lessons that physicality offers to our spirituality are ignored in favor of gross attachments to material possessions, sexual relationships, power and other such potent lures.

I-go has treated this planet to some rough justice. Billions of people live in a fearful state of mind and at a future point in time, worrying about the next meal, the next wage packet, the next bill to be paid, their children's health and safety etc. Eighty per cent of humanity live on less than $10 USD per day,[13] nearly a billion people entered the 21st century unable to read a book or sign their names[14] and in the year 2000, less than 1 per cent of what the world spent every year on weapons was needed to put every child into school.[15] Inequality is such that by 2004 about 0.13 per cent of the world's population controlled 25 per cent of the world's financial assets.[16]

These are not conditions primed to release spiritual attachments and repay energetic debt. Indeed, they are conditions ripe for i-go to flourish, people to be reborn, populations to soar, pressure on the planet's ecosystem to expand and life on earth to be pushed to the brink of extinction. Thus, humanity's own free will is quickly shepherding the species towards a final make-or-break choice between physical attachments and spiritual liberation. For centuries we have been choosing to listen to our i-go-tistical impulses and ignore a different natural urge to share and cooperate with the rest of the tribe. It is time for that impulse to change.

The planet earth, the ultimate we-go from which we are all made and to which we are all intrinsically connected and dependent, is threatening to reduce the population of our species if we are unable to do so ourselves through a process of spiritual enlightenment. Water shortages, land erosion, pollution, reduction of biodiversity, destructive environmental events and other natural and human-influenced phenomena are increasingly signaling the challenge before us: provolve or face consequences of your own making! If humanity is unable or unwilling to make the conscious choice to share, to nurture one another, to provide for the needs of people as a matter of course and to seek a collective answer to the pressing problems that we face as a spiritual species, the planet will simply thin the physical species and solve the problem on our behalf. It will reduce the number of bodies available for us to be born into. Global destruction is not just a physical event; it is a spiritual threshold chosen by self-ignorance, self-denial and obsession with physical desires and aversions.

If Provolution has been about one thing, it has ultimately been about the imperative of the personal reconnection to we-go by each individual i-go. Personal introspection, meditation, the cultivation of concentration and awareness, the discovery of self love and respect and practices of individual spiritual provolution all help to re-calibrate the energetic profile of your physical, mental and spiritual forms and this engenders a new future for us all. As you raise your energetic vibration you contribute to raising the energetic vibration of the collective we-go, which makes it easier for everyone else around you to do the same. Just as the constant creation of more and more forms of suffering facilitates an energetic environment where more people suffer more frequently, so your personal expansion of spiritual energy affects thoughts, words and behaviors around you and renders the environment more conducive to the spiritual liberation of all.

It does not take the creation of a machine to remove CO_2 from the atmosphere to save the planet from human ignorance; it takes the will of those individual people who are aware of their connectivity and dependence to assume responsibility for it. If you wish to assume responsibility for something greater than yourself you must first assume responsibility for the state of something as awesome as your '***self***' and all it implies. You are an energetic element of this planet and what you do affects everyone. What you think is imprinted upon the collective consciousness. What you provolve changes everything. No one and nothing outside of you can control that. It is yours to choose what you do with your own energetic creative force. Whether you live in a prison in Siberia or a tropical island in the Pacific, you are free in those terms. When you unleash internal freedom and feel its empowering energy, you will never again relinquish it to mind rafts that look like freedom but are made of chains, that talk of enlightenment but reside in darkness or that speak of liberty but assert control. You will know the difference for in self-contemplation you wake up, you unchain your potential and you live by universal laws, every one of which you will have experienced within your own spirit. You are the guide. You know the way home.

In order to evolve we need an expansion of consciousness, not aggression. Provolution does not occur by conquering land, seizing power or reclaiming the illusory icons of control. These are the tools of i-go and their day has passed. True power is found inside and begins with the awareness that i-go conditions you to repeat the suffering that you endure life after life and you no longer need it. If you are to change your future, to extinguish the conditions ensuring your physical rebirth and to simultaneously elevate the energetic profile of the collective we-go, you must become an explorer of your human spirit; the unmapped space in your heart that reveals far more about the universe than peering into the distant cosmos or at the smallest particles in a

Hadron Collider. This path requires no physical force. You need simply unleash the strength to be weak, the courage to be vulnerable and the faith to be free from the constant urge to be afraid of the intangible. In sensitivity and awareness, the journey of life requires nothing more than the effort to choose, the time to ripen and the mind rafts accepting that the journey is all there is to be had. You have nowhere to go. There is nothing to become. In uni-time, here and now and empowered with the sensitivity to sooth all suffering, your personal journey begins and ends with the discovery of your unique self, interconnected and interdependent with everything else in the universe.

That is provolution worth fighting for.

References

(1) Baumgartner, Richard N., Wang, Jack, Heymsfield, Steven B., Pierson, Richard N., Jr., Lichtman, Steven, Kamen, Yakov, Aliprantis, Antonios, "Body composition of technical complexity, and radiation exposure", American Journal of Clinical Nutrition - 1990 American Society for Clinical Nutrition, Inc.

(2) Jennifer L. Ruth, MD and Steven J. Wassner, MD, "Body Composition: Salt and Water" Pediatrics in Review. 2006; 27:181-188, American Academy of Pediatrics

(3) "More Money for Health Research but Better Focused", Global Forum for Health Research Press Release, P1, Nov 2004

(4) Eric G. Campbell, Ph.D., Russell L. Gruen, M.D., Ph.D., James Mountford, M.D., Lawrence G. Miller, M.D., Paul D. Cleary, Ph.D., and David Blumenthal, M.D., M.P.P., "A National Survey of Physician–Industry Relationships", New England Journal of Medicine, V 356:1742-1750, April 2007

(5) Gary Null PhD, Carolyn Dean MD ND, Martin Feldman MD, Debora Rasio MD and Dorothy Smith PhD, "Death by Medicine", Nutrition Institute of America, October 2003

(6) Robert S. Wilson, PhD; Kristin R. Krueger, PhD; Steven E. Arnold, MD; Julie A. Schneider, MD; Jeremiah F. Kelly, MD; Lisa L. Barnes, PhD; Yuxiao Tang, PhD; David A. Bennett, MD, "Loneliness and Risk of Alzheimer Disease", Arch Gen Psychiatry. 2007;64(2):234-240

(7) Cohen, Bernard L., "Catalog of Risks Extended and Updated", Health Physics 1991 Sept;61(3):317-335

(8) Cohen Sheldon, Doyle WJ, Skoner DP, Rabin BS and Gwaltney JM, "Social Ties and Susceptibility to the Common Cold", JAMA 227(24):1940-1944, 1997

(9) Kaprio J, Koskenvuo M, Rita H., "Mortality after bereavement: a prospective study of 95,647 widowed persons", American Journal of Public Health, 1987 Mar;77(3):283-7,

(10) SA Everson, DE Goldberg, GA Kaplan, RD Cohen, E Pukkala, J Tuomilehto and JT Salonen, "Hopelessness and Risk of Mortality and Incidence of Myocardial Infarction and Cancer", Psychosomatic Medicine, Vol 58, Issue 2 113-121, 1996

(11) Christian LM, Graham JE, Padgett DA, Glaser R, Kiecolt-Glaser JK, "Stress and Wound Healing", Lancet 1995;346:1194-1196

(12) David B. Barrett, et al., "World Christian Encyclopedia : A Comparative Survey of Churches and Religions in the Modern World," Oxford University Press, (2001), ISBN-13: 978-0195079630

(13) Martin Ravallion, Shaohua Chen and Prem Sangraula, "Dollar a day revisited", World Bank, May 2008. They note that 95 per cent of developing country population lived on less than $10 a day. Using 2005 population numbers, this is equivalent to just under 79.7 per cent of world population, and does not include populations living on less than $10 a day from industrialized nations.

(14) Carol Bellamy, "The state of the world's children", 1999, UNICEF

(15) Chris Brazier, "State of the World" New Internationalist Issue 287 - Feb 1997,

(16) Eileen Alt Powell, "Some 600,000 join millionaire ranks in 2004", Associate Press, June 9, 2005

BOOKS

O is a symbol of the world, of oneness and unity. In different cultures it also means the "eye," symbolizing knowledge and insight. We aim to publish books that are accessible, constructive and that challenge accepted opinion, both that of academia and the "moral majority."

Our books are available in all good English language bookstores worldwide. If you don't see the book on the shelves ask the bookstore to order it for you, quoting the ISBN number and title. Alternatively you can order online (all major online retail sites carry our titles) or contact the distributor in the relevant country, listed on the copyright page.

See our website **www.o-books.net** for a full list of over 500 titles, growing by 100 a year.

And tune in to myspiritradio.com for our book review radio show, hosted by June-Elleni Laine, where you can listen to the authors discussing their books.

MySpiritRadio